Landscapes of
SICILY

a countryside guide
Fourth edition

Peter Amann

D1297274

SUNFLOWER BOOKS

Fourth © 2013, reprinted 2014
Sunflower Books™
PO Box 36160
London SW7 3WS, UK
www.sunflowerbooks.co.uk

ISBN 978-1-85691-437-6

Vulcano's Gran Cratere (Walk 12)

Important note to the reader

We have tried to ensure that the descriptions and maps in this book are error-free at press date. The book will be updated, where necessary, whenever future printings permit. It will be very helpful for us to receive your comments (sent in care of the publishers, please) for the updating of future printings, and for the Update service described on the inside front cover of the book.

We also rely on those who use this book — especially walkers — to take along a good supply of common sense when they explore. Conditions change fairly rapidly on Sicily, and *storm damage or bulldozing may make a route unsafe at any time*. If the route is not as we outline it here, and your way ahead is not secure, return to the point of departure. *Never attempt to complete a tour or walk under hazardous conditions!* Please read carefully the notes on pages 45 to 48, as well as the introductory comments at the beginning of each tour and walk (regarding road conditions, equipment, grade, distances and time, etc). Explore *safely*, while at the same time respecting the beauty of the countryside.

www.walksicily.de, www.italien-aktiv.info
At the author's websites shown above you'll find up-to-date nformation about the walks in this book, GPS tracks for most of :m and many more tips for hotels and restaurants, as well as links ther websites of interest if you are walking in Sicily.

Cover: Cefalù from the castle rock (Car tour 4, Walk 19)
Title page: Pahoehoe lava on Mount Etna (Walk 6)

Photographs: Peter Amann
Maps: Sunflower Books, based on the 1:25,000 and 1:50,000 of the Istituto Geografico Militare, the Touring Club Italiano, and others
A CIP catalogue record for this book is available from the British Library.
Printed and bound in England: Short Run Press, Exeter

Contents

Preface

Speaking metaphorically, the landscape is the key that opens the door to a deeper understanding of Sicily. The fascination I feel for this island of endless variety has not left me from the moment I first set foot there in 1993. Since that time, I've spent the equivalent of several years travelling around Sicily. Many books have been written about the island; understandably, the majority of them deal with art history and archaeology. Others offer advice on the 'right' way to experience Sicily. Yet travel can be seen as a high art which calls for a more unhurried pace than is the norm in our present age of highly-developed tourism. Keeping in mind that time is a precious commodity, this book is an invitation to rediscover the leisure that allows travel the chance to become a true journey.

On a tour of Sicily the landscape is generally regarded as a sort of stage setting, and this setting is certainly magnificent. After all, the landscape can reveal as much about a region, its people and their history as an ancient temple. And of course, isn't one of the aesthetic pleasures of viewing a temple the way it is integrated into its surroundings?

Sicily is full of surprises. Its highest mountain is, at the same time, an active volcano — the largest in Europe. With eruptions occurring at regular intervals, Etna constantly makes its presence felt. Fortunately, there is no danger to human life. Etna is a rather 'peaceful' volcano, not an explosive fire mountain. Towering over all other Sicilian mountains by more than 1300m/4250ft, the volcano at its summit reaches an elevation of 3300m/10,825ft. Climbing Etna takes one through varied climatic zones, each with its own distinctive vegetation. It is almost like taking a trip from Palermo to the North Pole. Subtropical orange and lemon groves give way to stands of oak and the southernmost beech forests in Europe. Up to an elevation of 2500m/8200ft, the ground is covered by a layer of thorny shrubs known locally as *spino santo (Astragalus siculus)*. Lava beds void of all plant life extend from here to the peak, which is covered with snow for much of the year. In 1987, Etna became a regional park and was placed under environmental protection.

The ancient theatre of Taormina provides the frame for the classic view of Etna and the Bay of Naxos. Famous Taormina is a small town located in the foothills of the Monti Peloritani. These mountains, with their jagged peaks and wide valleys, are the geological continuation of the Calabrian Aspromonte, separated only by the narrow Straits of Messina.

In the Tyrrhenian Sea, off the northern coast of Sicily, lie the Aeolian Islands, a UNESCO World Heritage Site. The archipelago forms a volcanic bridge which extends from Etna to Vesuvius at the Gulf of Naples: seven volcanic islands, two of which, Lipari and Vulcano, are described in this book.

A chain of mountains runs along Sicily's northern coast: the Peloritani in the east, followed by the Nebrodi and the Madonie. In 1993 Sicily established a regional park in the forest-covered Nebrodi range. These mountains are characterised by their gently-undulating contours, in spite of the fact that the highest peak is over 1800m/5900ft in elevation. However, where limestone deposits begin to emerge, as they do at Alcara li Fusi, the landscape becomes much more dramatic. The Madonie mountain range, which became a regional park back in 1989, consists of rocky limestone mountains whose forests are home to the richest variety of plant life in the Mediterranean.

These limestone mountains continue to the west. The Conca d'Oro and Palermo are both encircled by mountains, while barren peaks protect the Zingaro park from the raw west wind and allow dwarf palms to flourish. The Egadi Islands, off the coast of Trapani, seem to have been tossed haphazardly into the ocean. Looming out of the water like a stone ship, the island of Marettimo keeps its lonely vigil, impassively resisting the pounding of the waves. The remainder of Sicily's west coast slopes gradually into the ocean and is in many ways reminiscent of the shores of North Africa. The ancient man-made landscape of the salt flats located between Trapani and Marsala is an endless source of fascination.

Sicily's interior is associated with many clichés: donkey carts; widows dressed in black in the streets and alleys; men, their flat caps askew on their heads, with sawn-off shotguns under their arms. These images are still perpetrated in popular films and block-buster novels. In contrast, the younger generation in towns like San Guiseppe Iato, Prizzi and Corleone is trying to create a future for itself without the Mafia. Yet a portion of the landscape remains unchanged since Roman antiquity, and durum wheat ripens each year on the golden hills of Sicily's interior.

Southeastern Sicily is a place of light. Rivers have carved out canyons in the chalky Monti Iblei (a future national park), and in summer they are lined with a profusion of flowering oleanders. On the plains above, kilometres of stone walls pattern the landscape. In aeons past, the limestone tables of the Iblei, Apulia and the Aegean Islands formed one continuous geological mass. It is fascinating to think that hundreds of thousands of years after the ancient Greeks emigrated west, they came to settle once again on their own soil.

The *primavera siciliana* is proverbial, with the hills covered in a lavish display of flowers. Less well known is that a second 'spring' occurs in autumn after the long dry summer. Although the rainy season begins in the middle of November, there are still beautiful days in January. Those illustrious Europeans who until 70 years ago spent their winters in Taormina did so with good reason.

Well into the 1950s, the *carretti siciliani* (mule-drawn carts) were the most common form of transport for those who lived in the country. Just as the *carretti* have been replaced by the *ape* (motorised tricycles) and modern vehicles, agricultural practices have also undergone great change. Agriculture continues to play an important role in Sicily, but today highly-advanced farming methods are used. The old stone-paved mule tracks have either lost their significance and are slowly crumbling, or are partially paved in asphalt. This has not always been done out of necessity, but often merely because the work could be paid for with public funds. Some of the paths described in this book were in use hundreds, if not thousands of years ago. Their preservation is just as important as that of a temple or a medieval church.

Hiking can help to maintain the cultural landscape. The local population often sees measures aimed at protecting nature as patronising. But if by preserving the old routes, we can give the landscape a new economic importance, then we will have gained a great deal. Mimmo Lombardo, formerly of the AAPIT Palermo and now of the Centro Regionale per la Progettazione e il Restauro in Palermo, along with his task force, has done this most effectively. Within my limited means, I am attempting to do the same. I have written this book as your invitation to discover one of the most varied landscapes in Europe on foot, while becoming acquainted with the people and their history.

After all, didn't Odysseus, the greatest traveller of all, honour the island with his presence? *Benvenuti in Sicilia!*

Recommended reading

This book is a practical guide to the landscapes of Sicily. The following books will give you a deeper appreciation of the people, their history, art and culture.

Andrews, Robert and Jules Brown: *Sicily, The Rough Guide* (Rough Guides)
Norwich, John Julius: *The Normans in the South* (Penguin)
Robb, Peter: *Midnight in Sicily* (Faber & Faber)
Simeti, Mary Taylor: *On Persephone's Island* (Vintage)

Acknowledgements

Researching a travel guide is always a major undertaking, but in Sicily it is an adventure … and an addictive one at that. I would first like to thank my publisher, Pat Underwood, who made this book possible. Of the many friends, both old and new, who accompanied me or pointed me in the right direction, provided hospitality or valuable tips, I would like to thank at least a few by name: Gundula Anders, Stefania d'Angelo, Carlo and Corrado Assenza, Nino Barcia, Bruno Biondo, Salvatore and Marina Bonajuto, Jenny Bond, Mimmo Caputo, Brigit and Jasmin Carnabuci, Rino Causapruno, Luigi Cordio, Nuccio Faro, Matteo Feretti, Vincenzo Fiocco, Gaetano Geraci, Giovanni Giardina, Melo and Enrico Gallodoro, Nicola and Illuminata Granà, Mimmo Lombardo, Ignazio Maiorana, Meredith Menzel, Vito Oddo, Antonio Presti, Charlie and Shirley Sacamano, Gerardo Schuler, Salvatore Speranza, Giuseppe Spina, Pierfilippo Spoto, Giuseppe Tirito, Stephen Tobriner, Giovanna and Paolo Tornabene, and last but not least Marisin and Salvatore Tranchina. *Questo libro è dedicato a Voi!*

Getting about

If you have enough time and patience — the magic word is *pazienza* — almost any town or village in Sicily can be reached by **train** or **bus**. Schedules are printed in the newspapers and online. But some of the interesting archaeological excavations and almost all of the walks are difficult to reach by public transport (if it *is* possible to do so, this has been noted in the relevant walk). If your time is limited, and you want to discover Sicily on foot — and at your own pace — a **car** is indispensable.

You can travel to Sicily by car: driving down Italy's 'boot' is time-consuming, but most enjoyable. Alternatives are **overnight ferries** like the Grandi Navi Veloci line from Genoa to Palermo, SNAV from Naples to the Aeolian Islands or Palermo, Tirrenia from Naples to Palermo and TTL lines from Naples to Catania. A day ferry connects Salerno with Messina (see 'Useful addresses', page 50).

All of the major car rental companies (*Noleggio Auto*) have offices at the Palermo and Catania airports. Vehicles can also be rented in most of the provincial capitals. There is an especially large selection in Cefalù, Giardini Naxos and Taormina.

There are a number of pleasant **train** journeys, such as that along the coast from Trapani to Messina, and further on to Syracuse. Don't miss the journey between Syracuse and Ragusa! A trip on the **narrow-gauge Circumetnea railway** (see 'Useful addresses', page 50) is a wonderful experience. Departing from Catania or Giarre-Riposto, the train rounds Etna several times a day. The stretch between Catania and Giarre is served by the FS state railway.

The Aeolian Islands are best reached by **ferry** or **hydrofoil** from Milazzo. The Egadi Islands are best approached from Trapani (see 'Useful addresses', page 50). You can do without a car on the islands (and in many cases, cars are not permitted).

Tonnara di Scopello (Car tour 5)

☀ *Picnicking* ────────────

There are many official picnic areas in Sicily, often established by the forestry service. Unfortunately, many of these sites are just off the road and have no views. On weekends, Sicilians enjoy a *scampagnata*, a family outing where everyone eats together in the fresh air … and the company is more important than the scenery.

The 27 suggestions listed here are either particularly attractive official picnic areas or idyllic spots which can quickly be reached on foot. They are indicated on the touring maps and relevant walking maps by the symbol *P* printed in green.

Fresh fruit and vegetables are available throughout the year. Good Sicilian bread, with a distinctive yellowish tint, is made from durum wheat. The cheese from the Madonie, Nebrodi and Iblei mountains is especially delicious. Good sausages are made in the Madonie and Nebrodi as well. The Sicilians share with the Italians a passion for good spring water. You'll often see whole families stocking up at the wells, filling bottles and canisters. A must for dessert is *pasta di mandorla*, an almond cake which every pastry shop bakes according to its own recipe.

Sicilians like to eat out, and we should follow their example. Thanks to the legacy of Greek, Punic, Roman, Arabic and Spanish invaders, the Sicilian cuisine is varied and extensive. Once could say that, in Sicily, history goes via the kitchen directly to the stomach.

All picnickers should read the country code on page 47 and go quietly in the countryside.

1 MONTI ROSSI (touring map/map page 51, photograph page 51) 🛱
Car tour 1: The **Pineta di Monti Rossi** (833m/2730ft) is an *area attrezzata* (official picnic site) at the northern edge of Nicolosi. It is open daily from 08.00-19.30 in summer and from 09.00-17.00 in winter (1 € entrance fee, www.pinetamonti rossi.com. There are picnic tables, barbecues and toilets. Pines provide shade, and there is a view to Mount Etna. An easy walk leads from here or behind the campground up to the rim of the **Monti Rossi** crater (Walk 1).

2 PIAN DEL VESCOVO (touring map) 🛱
Car tour 1: There are some picnic tables at the **Pian del Vescovo** (1376m/ 4515ft), shaded by trembling aspens *(Populus tremula)*. Another good spot can be reached after a short walk (2.3km/1.5mi; 45min) into the **Vallone degli Zappini**, the valley that leads north to La Montagnola. The path ends under a large beech tree, by the **Acqua della Rocca** (one of the very few springs on Etna) in a little cave. This place used to be frequented by the local shepherds.

3 CASA PIETRACANNONE (touring map/map pages 58-59, photo page 55) 🛱
Car tour 1: Park on the Strada Mareneve, then walk down the cart track to the **Casa Pietracannone** (1150m/3770ft). The house stands on old lava, which had engulfed an ancient, weathered tree-trunk. The hole remaining resembles a

Above: Cave di Cusa (Picnic 17); right: ancient olive tree at the Hera temple in Agrigento (Car tour 6). Opposite page: Giardino Ibleo in Ragusa Ibla (left, Picnic 26); theatre in Morgantina (top right, Picnic 22); picnic site in S. Martino delle Scale, with a view to Pizzo del Corvo (bottom right, Picnic 14).

cannon and gave the house its name. Picnic tables have been set in the abandoned apple orchard under big Etna broom. You can buy groceries in Milo or S. Alfio. In autumn fresh fruit is sold by street vendors. The Casa Pietracannone is the starting point for Walk 3.

4 ROCCA NOVARA (touring map/map page 78, photograph page 20)
Car tour 2: You don't have to climb the peak of **Rocca Novara** (Walk 14) to enjoy the splendid views over Novara di Sicilia, the Tyrrhenian coast and the Aeolian Islands. Just follow the walk to the saddle reached in 25min, where there are good places to sit. You can buy everything you need for your picnic in Novara di Sicilia.

5 CUBA DI S. DOMENICA (touring map)
Car tour 2: Driving from Francavilla towards Castiglione, a track branches off to the right immediately after the bridge over the Alcantara River. Park here. Follow the track over a footbridge and upstream, then turn right immediately, down to the river. Where the gas pipe crosses the river, step over the drystone wall on your left. Follow the main path, which eventually bends to the left, and go right at the crossing track shortly after. At the next crossing go left, to the **Cuba** (ruins of a lovely medieval Byzantine church). From the small hilltop you'll enjoy a fine view of Mount Etna and Castiglione di Sicilia. The **little gorges of the Alcantara** are just a few steps away. Return the same way (2km/1.2mi; 40min). You can also get close to the Cuba by car. From the road to Castiglione, turn right towards Randazzo at the Bivio Galuzzo, and follow signs to the Cuba.

6 MARINA DI COTTONE (touring map)
Car tour 2: From Fiumefreddo drive 3km to the pleasant pebble beach of **Marina di Cottone**, at the mouth of the Fiumefreddo River. A nature reserve, the Oasi di Fiumefreddo, is nearby — apart from the Ciane River near Syracuse (Walk 36), the only place in Sicily to see papyrus growing wild. Linguaglossa, Piedimonte Etneo or Fiumefreddo are good places to shop for your picnic.

7 SOLAZZO (map pages 80-81)
Car tour 3: In spite of its low height, the **Solazzo** peak (1530m/1518ft) is one of the best viewpoints in the Nebrodi. The peak is easily reached in 30 minutes from the **Portella Femmina Morta** (see Shorter walk 15). Sandstone rocks make good seats, oaks offer shade, and the view to Mount Etna is marvellous.

8 CHRISTO SIGNOR DELLA MONTAGNA (touring map)

Car tour 3: The town of **Cesarò** is dominated by a larger-than-life statue of Christ, rising on a sandstone rock. Follow the signs 'Christo Signor della Montagna' out of the town centre, past the Hotel dei Nebrodi and a couple of grocer's shops. Turn right along Via Piturro and park beneath the rock. Steps take you to the top in about five minutes. On a clear day the 360° panorama is breathtaking.

9 CASTELLO NELSON MANIACE (touring map, photograph page 23) ⊼

Car tour 3: There are tree-shaded picnic tables in front of the **Castello Nelson Maniace**, as well as a children's playground, and toilets inside the castle (during opening hours: daily from 09.00-13.00 and 14.30 until sunset; 1 € entrance fee).

10 CASTLE ROCK OF CEFALÙ (touring map/map page 90, photographs pages 88, 90 and cover) ⊼

Car tour 4: A clearly-marked path leads from Cefalù up to the castle rock (Walk 19). After passing the **Tempio di Diana**, you come to a belvedere (30min) with a breathtaking view over the old town and the dome (open from 09.00 until one hour before sunset; an entrance fee is under consideration). There are plenty of well-stocked grocers in Cefalù, where you can buy any food for your picnic. Don't miss the excellent local cheese from the Madonie!

11 SANTUARIO DI GIBILMANNA (touring map)

Car tour 4: From the **Santuario**, past the museum entrance, the stone-paved Via del Calvario leads through an iron gate into the oak wood. After a couple of minutes you'll reach a little open air theatre and a semicircular stone bench, where the monks met to talk in the shade of the trees. Or you can go left, below the Santuario, following the *Sentiero Salvabosco* nature trail, until you come to some rocks with a splendid view over Cefalù, the sea and the Aeolian Islands (about 15 minutes' walking) .

12 BELVEDERE 'U CASTRU' IN PETRALIA SOPRANA (touring map)

Car tour 4: From the Piazza del Polpolo in Petralia Soprana the Via del Loreto leads past the eponymous church to the **Belvedere 'U Castru'**. The strategic importance of this place was recognised as early as the Bronze Age; it later became a Punic and then a Roman stronghold. The Normans built a castle on the same spot in the 11th century. There is a fine panorama, stretching over much of inland Sicily and beyond Gangi to Mount Etna.

13 PICNIC IN PALERMO (touring map)

Car tour 5: Even in the middle of frenetic Palermo you can find a quiet corner to retreat for a picnic. The **Giardino Inglese** at the Via Libertà, the **Giardino Garibaldi** on the Piazza Marina, or the **Villa Giulia** near the Botanical Gardens are good places. But before you settle down, first be sure to buy some picnic delicacies at one of the oriental street markets like the Ballarò or Capo.

14 S. MARTINO DELLE SCALE (touring map/map page 102, photographs pages 11, 102) ⊼

Car tour 5: There is a small picnic area above **S. Martino delle Scale**. The tables are set in the shade of pines and there is a fine view over the Conca d'Oro, Palermo and Pizzo del Corvo. Buy your food in Palermo's street markets, fill your canteens with fresh water in Boccadifalco (like the Sicilians do) and get your delicious fresh durum wheat bread in S. Martino delle Scale itself. Other nice places for a picnic are the peak of **Pizzo del Corvo** (Walk 25) or the **Belvedere** in **Monreale**.

15 PARCO DELLO ZINGARO (touring map/map page 105, photograph page 107) ⊼

Car tour 5: One of Sicily's most beautiful picnic areas lies at the southern entrance to the **Parco dello Zingaro** nature reserve (Walk 27). Tables are set just above the sea, and there are barbecues with fire wood. On weekends, mainly during summer, many people from Palermo come here to enjoy a family outing.

16 ISOLA DI MOZIA (touring map, photograph page 15)

Car tour 5: A few kilometres north of Marsala, a boat leaves from the jetty at the Salina Ettore salt flat for the island of **Mozia** (every half hour, with an break between 13.00 to 15.00). The trip costs about 5 euros, and you have to pay a fee to visit the island and the little museum (www.fondazionewhitaker.it). There are plenty of pretty picnic spots on this little island. There are toilets near the Villa Whitaker (archaeological museum).

17 CAVE DI CUSA (touring map, photograph page 10, top left)

Car tour 5: The **Cave di Cusa** are ancient stone quarries a few kilometres southwest of Campobello di Mazara. While picnicking in archaeological sites is officially prohibited, the guardians won't mind if you find a nice place in the shade of an olive tree. From the car park, follow the gravel track past the barrier. Dunes, consolidated into sandstone, form a low ridge running from east to west. In ancient times, the Greeks of Selinunte quarried this stone to build their temples.

You can stroll beside the banks of the Ciane in dappled sunlight (Walk 36) and enjoy a picnic in the midst of papyrus (Picnic 23).

18 THE FICUZZA PALACE GARDEN (touring map/map pages 112-113) ⚲

Car tour 6: Behind the palace of **Ficuzza** there's a wild garden stretching to the woods, with tree-shaded picnic tables and benches. The place is very popular on weekends, when families come from nearby Palermo. If the weather turns bad, you can always get a good simple meal in the Bar Cavaretta in Ficuzza. The area is famous for its sausages and cheese. For great food try the Antica Stazione di Ficuzza or the more rustic Rifugio Alpe Cucco (Walks 30, 31).

19 FORTRESS OF THE OAKS (touring map)

Car tour 6: **Caltabelotta** lies on a jagged mountain 949m/3113ft above the coastal plain. The Arabs called the place Qal'at al-Balluth ('fortress of the oaks'). Three rocky peaks tower over the old town. From the Chiesa Madre you can reach a number of breathtaking viewpoints. On a clear day the view stretches over dozens of hill towns, from Mount Erice to Etna. The ruins of the old castle can be reached after just a short scramble. Buy your food in Caltabelotta.

20 CAPO BIANCO (touring map/map pages 118-119, photograph page 119)

Car tour 6: For a beach picnic, nothing beats **Eraclea Minoa**'s bay at **Capo Bianco**. You can drive all the way down to the beach (Walk 33). If you don't want to picnic, both the Lido Gabbiano and the Sabbia d'Oro serve good fish.

21 SICILY'S UMBILICUS (touring map)

Car tour 7: The town of **Enna** lies just at the geographical centre of Sicily — 'Sicily's umbilicus' to the ancient Greeks. East of the Castello di Lombardia lies the **Rocca di Cerere**. The main sanctuary of the fertility goddess Demeter (later the Roman Ceres), stood on these rocks. The temple has disappeared, but the splendid view remains. If it's windy, you can shelter in one of the castle courtyards (WC). On weekdays mornings, a market is held south of the Via Roma in Enna: upholding the reputation of Demeter, it is famous for its excellent bread!

22 MORGANTINA — MONTE CITADELLA (touring map, photo page 11)

Car tour 7: South of the ticket booth (wc) for the **Scavi di Morgantina** there's a low hill offering a fine view over the ancient town, the surrounding countryside and Mount Etna. You can sit on rocks to picnic. Looking out east over the excavations, you'll see Monte Citadella. If you follow the forestry track alongside the perimeter fence of the archaeological site, you'll reach a saddle on the western slope of Monte Citadella, where the track runs north and south to circle the hill. On the eastern side of **Monte Citadella**, in the midst of the ancient walls, there is another pleasant picnic spot with fine views (4km/2.5mi; 1h).

23 CIANE RIVER (touring map/map page 124, photograph pages 12-13)

Car tour 8: The stroll along the **Ciane River** (Walk 36) is ideal for picnickers. Buy your food in Syracuse at the market which is held every weekday morning on the Ortigia promontory. If you are looking for a good wine as well, try the Fratelli Burgio Slow Food-Deli, Piazza Batisti 4, tel.: 0931600069, www.saporiburgio.com.

24 NOTO ANTICA (touring map/map page 126, photograph page 125) ⊼

Car tour 8: The official picnic area lies north of the mighty city walls, but you'll find plenty of nice spots with fine views to the bastion of **Noto Antica** itself (Walk 37). The grocers' shops in Noto have all your picnic needs. Be sure to try the local *pasta di mandorla* for dessert (my favourite place is Caffè Sicilia)!

25 PARCO FORZA (touring map) ⊼

Car tour 8: The **Parco Forza**, the location of ancient Ispica, is situated east of the modern town (open daily from 09.00 until one hour before sunset). While some old walls and ancient necropoli have survived, it is the *view* you have come to see. From the parking area a stone-paved road descends past the Trattoria Greenway to the **Cava d'Ispica**. Once you have reached the bottom of the valley, there are more picnic spots in the shade of walnut trees or on sun-warmed rocks. The church of **S. Maria della Cava** lies to your right; behind its baroque façade there's a hidden Byzantine oratory hewn in the rock. From here a path climbs all the way up the Cava d'Ispica to the **Larderia Necropoli** (26km/16mi; 8h). The path isn't always viable for the whole way, but go up as far as you like, and you'll find nice places to stop for a picnic. The Larderia Necropoli can be reached by car as well (see Car tour 8, page 42).

26 RAGUSA IBLA — GIARDINO IBLEO (touring map/map page 131, photographs pages 11, 130-131

Car tour 8: At the eastern end of **Ragusa Ibla** lies the **Giardino Ibleo**, a perfect viewpoint towards the upper Irminio Valley. On Saturdays you might be lucky enough to see some beautifully-dressed brides having their pictures taken in the pretty surroundings of this park. In the local grocer's shops you should find everything you need for a picnic, but the local cuisine in the many restaurants is tempting too.

27 PANTALICA — ANAKTORON (touring map/map page 134, photograph page 132)

Car tour 8: Even if you don't want to hike in Pantalica (Walk 41), the short drive from Ferla is worthwhile. Sitting at the **Anaktoron**, the ruins of an Bronze Age palace, with some good bread, cheese and wine, you can easily imagine yourself back in ancient times. The Trattoria Pantalica Paradise at Contrada Filiporto on the road from Ferla to the Anaktoron, offers good food in a simple setting from April to October (mobile: 3929946230).

Touring

With more than 25,000 square kilometres, Sicily is the largest region in Italy and the biggest island in the Mediterranean. The eight suggested car tours (covering almost 2000km) not only take in all the important places and the most beautiful sites, but afford an overview of Sicily's immense variety of landscapes. Realistically, you will probably only be able to cover two or three of these tours in a single holiday, especially if you want to walk as well.

Most of the **roads** in Sicily are well built, and the tours follow little-used secondary roads as much as possible, taking you to places well off the beaten track and emphasising possibilities for **walking** and **picnicking**. All the picnic and walk suggestions either lie on the main routes or are reached via short detours.

Take care to fill up with **petrol** regularly, as it is against the law in Italy to carry reserve fuel. As a rule, petrol stations are closed from 12.30 to 15.00 and from 22.00 until 07.00, but at self-service stations you can fill up 24 hours a day — so carry a couple of unwrinkled 10 or 20 euro bills with you.

With one exception, all tours are written up as circuits, beginning and ending in places that are particularly interesting and good bases for short or long visits. At appropriate intervals the *cumulative distance* covered is given in kilometres (all signposting is in kilometres).

The pull-out touring map is designed to be held out opposite the touring notes and contains all the information you will need outside the towns. The **symbols** used in the touring notes correspond to those on the touring map and are explained on the map key.

View from the Imbarcadero di Mozia over the salt pans of Trapani, with Monte Erice rising in the background (Car tour 5)

Car tour 1: AROUND MOUNT ETNA

Catania (centre) • Nicolosi • Rifugio Sapienza • Piano Provenzana • Bronte • Adrano • Catania (ring road)

159km/99mi; 5-6 hours' driving (allow at least one day for this tour)

On route: Picnics (see pages 9-14) 1-3; Walks 1-8 (with accommodation tips)

The circuit starts in Catania and rounds Mount Etna on well-built roads. On the Strada Mareneve between Fornazzo and Linguaglossa you must carry snow chains between December 1st and March 31st.

On this tour you will discover the many faces of Europe's highest active volcano. From sea level at Catania the road rises to almost 2000m and crosses several vegetational zones, from the subtropical to the alpine. Like any active volcano, Etna is a dynamic mountain and is subject to permanent change. The eruptions in 1991-92 completely filled the Valle del Bove with fresh lava, and continuous eruptions since 1998 have given the Cratere di Sud-Est (one of the four summit craters) its prominent cone. In 2003 Piano Provenzana was partly covered by lava.

Leave the centre of **Catania★** (*i*✝︎**ⅠⅠ**✹**▲▲**✕️**▣**⊕︎❀︎**M**) on the basalt-cobbled Via Etnea, making straight towards Mount Etna. The villages of **Gravina** and **Mascalucia** (▲✕️▣) blend into each other. **Nicolosi★** (15km *i*✝︎▲▲✕️▣⊕︎) is a typical small town on the flanks of the mountain. The Parco dell'Etna has its headquarters here in the former Benedictine monastery of San Nicolò. Nicolosi lies at the foot of Monti Rossi, a crater which was formed during the 1669 eruption, when lava reached the city of Catania and partially destroyed it. At the northern end of the village you'll find the entrance to the **Pineta di Monti Rossi** (16km ⛺︎WC; Picnic 1), where Walk 1 begins and ends.

Continuing along the SP92 in direction of 'Etna Sud', the summit of Mount Etna rises ahead. Older and younger lava layers overlap, and numerous craters line the road. After the eruption of 1983, the road had to be rebuilt above the hotel La Nuova Quercia (23km ▲▲✕️). The new road cuts through the black and barren lava, which left only the occasional tree or little 'island' of woods in its wake. Lay-bys encourage short stops (📷). Looking back, the silhouette of the Monti Rossi stands out clearly. Shortly before the km17 road-marker, you could turn left towards the 'Grande Albergo' and the starting point of a nature trail, the *Sentiero Natura Monte Nero degli Zappini* (32km). Continuing on the SP92 (rebuilt after the flank eruptions of 2001-03) you reach the highest point of the tour at the **Rifugio Sapienza** (34km *i*▲▲🐾✕️WC). A cable car goes from here up to a height of 2504m/8213ft, from where you can either walk or take one of the SITAS jeeps up to the Torre del Filosofo (2919m/9574ft; Walk 2).

Do make a short stop in front of the **Crateri Silvestri** (35km 📷✕️WC), pretty craters which can easily be circled on foot. It is the classical 'hike' for most of the tourists from Taormina. From now on the road descends towards Zafferana. The landscape is painted in a broad palette of colours: pine woods and grass-covered slopes alternate with black or reddish cinder slopes, and yellow-flowering Etna broom *(Ginesta aetnensis)* flourishes in late summer. The road leads past the **Pian del Vescovo**, a little plain (39km 📷🎌; Picnic 2). After three kilometres you could take a detour on a cul-de-sac road to Monte Pomiciaro (📷; +10km there and back). From the turning place at the top you would enjoy an excellent view into the Valle del Bove and the 1991-92 lava flow.

Approaching Zafferana Etnea you'll see the lava flow which threatened the village in 1992. From **Zafferana Etnea** (50km ⛪🏔 ✕🚾) continue towards Milo, ascending through a beautiful forest of oaks. The vineyards on the right belong to the Baron di Villagrande. Beyond **Milo**, the road rises further, to the houses of **Fornazzo** (56km). The village of Sant' Alfio★ (*i*⛪🏔✕🚾) lies nearby.

Continue your tour along the Strada Mareneve, which starts here in Fornazzo and crosses the 1979 lava flow straight away. Gaining height, Etna's summit craters come into view again, this time from a new perspective. On a right-hand bend you pass the **Casa Pietracannone** (61km 📷🎌; Picnic 3; Walk 3). Shortly after, a road from Sant'Alfio and the *agriturismo* La Cirasella (🏔✕) comes up to join the Strada Mareneve. Beyond some chestnut groves the road runs through a turkey oak wood, the **Bosco Cerrita**. The first birches

Vineyards on the northern slopes of Mount Etna (top left) and flowing lava at the Cratere di Sud-Est (top right). Below: view from the Strada Mareneve above Sant'Alfio towards the summit craters

appear a little further up. The crest of the Serra delle Concazze, with the Pizzi Deneri (Walk 5), dominates the landscape up to the left. Turn left (68.5km) on a signposted cul-de-sac road, to the **Rifugio Citelli** (70.5km *i📷🏠✕🍴WC*) — a mountain hut (not always open; www.rifugiocitelli.com) and starting point of numerous walks (Walks 4 and 5).

Returning to the Strada Mareneve, you cross the broad lava flow of 1865; the Monti Sartorius (Walk 4), with their black cinder cones, rise to your left, while the mighty crater of Monte Nero (Walk 6) is ahead. The road starts to descend towards the fresh 2003 lava, and you reach a crossroads (72km): turn left, on a a cul-de-sac road to the **Piano Provenzana** (75km 📷🔺✕WC), a centre for winter sports and starting point of several walks (Walk 6; photograph page 61). STAR jeeps drive up towards Etna's summit craters from here.

The Strada Mareneve descends through tall pine woods towards Linguaglossa, passing a number of picnic sites and mountain huts (🍴🏠). Then the pines give way to oaks and chestnuts. Between the tree trunks you catch glimpses of the Peloritani range, Taormina and Linguaglossa. About 4km before Linguaglossa, turn left on a narrow road towards Bronte (90km). This road offers open views into the Alcantara Valley and towards the Peloritani and Nebrodi mountains. Shortly after the town of Randazzo comes into view for the first time, a cul-de-sac road off left (signalled by a lava rock inscribed 'Parco dell'Etna') leads down to the Case Pirao (102km; Walk 7). Continue straight ahead, crossing the 1981 lava flow. At the **Bivio Dagala Longa** crossroads (108km), turn left on the SS284 towards Bronte.

The road climbs effortlessly uphill past orchards and vineyards. Etna's summit craters are visible to the left, while the undulating Nebrodi stretch out to the right. The town of Troina stands out in the west like an eagles' nest above inland Sicily's plains of grain. At the northern entrance to **Bronte★** (117km *i🛉🔺✕🍴M*) you'll see a road signposted to the hotel Parco dell'Etna and restaurant Villa Etrusca. Then follow Viale Kennedy to the southeast; this cul-de-sac leads to the starting point for Walk 8. Even if you don't like hiking, this little diversion into a bizzare lava landscape is very worthwhile (+12km there and back).

Circle the old town of Bronte, following signs for Adrano and Catania; the Monti Erei are visible on the far side of the Simeto Valley. Turn off left for Adrano (133km); don't be put off by the ugly outskirts — the old town of **Adrano★** (135km 🛉🚻📷✕🍴🏧M) definitely merits a short visit.

Then continue the journey on the good SS284, through well-cultivated countryside. The gulf of Catania opens up ahead. Past **Paternò** (🚻🔺✕📷), pick up the SS121 expressway and follow it to **Misterbianco**, where you pick up the motorway ring road round **Catania** (159km). Here you can decide which way to continue your tour. If you are moving on to Taormina, the drive along the Riviera dei Ciclopi, past Acireale, is beautiful.

Car tour 2: TAORMINA, THE PELORITANI MOUNTAINS AND THE AEOLIAN ISLANDS

Taormina • (Forza d'Agrò • Alì) • Messina • Milazzo • (Lipari • Vulcano) • Milazzo • Novara di Sicilia • Castiglione di Sicilia • Linguaglossa • Fiumefreddo • Taormina

177km/110mi; about 5-6 hours' driving without detours. Suggested detours: Forza d'Agrò: 8km/5mi; 30min, Alì: 23km/14mi; 45min, Capo Milazzo: 12km/7mi; 30min, Tyndaris: 35km/22mi; 45min

On route: Picnics (see pages 9-14) 4-6; Walks 9-14 (with accommodation tips)

This tour through northeastern Sicily mainly follows well-built secondary roads. I suggest you use the motorway between Messina and Milazzo, to avoid some time-consuming driving through unattractive built-up areas. The port of Milazzo is the best base for reaching the Aeolian Islands. Vulcano and/or Lipari can also be visited on a day trip. To get the best out of this tour, try to stay overnight in Milazzo or nearby. Better still, plan a night or two on the islands! With the exception of Vulcano and Lipari, all the walks are accessible from Taormina.

Taormina hardly requires any introduction. The view from the Greco-Roman theatre towards the Bay of Naxos and Mount Etna is the picture-postcard image of Sicily. Today package-holiday tourists follow in the footsteps of the cultivated travellers of yesteryear. Miraculously, Taormina has lost none of its charm — at least if you avoid the summer months. The Peloritani Mountains occupy the northeastern tip of Sicily, the Nebrodi Mountains follow on in the west, and Etna rises to the south. The Nebrodi are the geological continuation of the Calabrian Aspromonte, separated only by the Strait of Messina. Sharp mountain ridges and the *fiumare* (valleys with broad gravel beds, that carry water only after the thaw or heavy rains) are typical of this landscape. Most of the once-cultivated terraces are now abandoned. The mountain roads are threatened by frequent landslides, and you will see much reafforestation, which has been introduced to prevent further erosion.

From **Taormina★** (🚶🚴🛏🍴🖼🏖🗻🚻⊕❄M; Walk 9) take the SS114 towards Messina, following a coast lined with numerous resorts. At **Capo S. Alessio** (10km) a road leads left to Forza d'Agrò★ (🛏🍴✗🖼), where Walk 10 begins (+8km return). I wholeheartedly recommend this detour at some point during your stay: the pretty mountain village has been the setting for a few films. Another lovely

Castiglione di Sicilia, with Mount Etna in the background

In the Peloritani — Rocca Novara (Walk 14)

day trip from Taormina is a circuit in the Agrò Valley: you could visit the Norman church of SS. Pietro e Paolo from either Scifì or Casalvecchio Siculo, and the small town of Sacova★ (☝✕▣) has a wonderful setting over the sea.

Continuing on the main tour, in **Alì Terme** (25km ▲) you pass the road off left to Alì (☝✕▣), the starting point for Walk 11 (+23km return). Continue on the SS114 to the motorway at **Messina Sud** (42km). Then I suggest you take the motorway (toll payable) as far as Milazzo. If you would like to visit Messina★ (☝☝▣▲△✕➾⊕M), take the exit 'Messina Centro' (48km).

The motorway pierces a long tunnel through the Peloritani Mountains, and suddenly you reappear on the Tyrrhenian coast. On a clear day some of the Aeolian Islands will already be in view. Milazzo announces itself with its long peninsula and refineries.

Leave the motorway at the **Milazzo/Isole Eolie exit** (69km) and follow the signs 'porto' to the port of **Milazzo★** (74km ☝☝▮▲ ▣✕➾⊕). Hydrofoils and ferries run several times a day between Milazzo and the Aeolian Islands (Walk 12 and 13). You can get tickets and timetables in the various agencies, all of which are situated on the Via dei Mille which runs along the harbour (see 'Useful addresses', page 50). Between April 3rd and October 31st, only residents and tourists with a permit can take their cars to the islands, but there are supervised garages in the Via G. Rizzo (a street running parallel with Via dei Mille), where you can leave your car for one or more days. Milazzo doesn't look very enticing at first, but if you spend a little time here, you'll be surprised. The old town lies at the feet of an imposing castle, which merits a visit. But it is also worth driving out to the tip of Capo di Milazzo, to enjoy the view to the Aeolian Islands (+12km return).

From **Milazzo** continue west along the SS113, initially through a heavily built-up area. A few kilometres past **Castroreale Terme**, you come to your turn-off: the SS185 (90km). But another rewarding detour (+35km return) is possible first: you could continue to Tyndaris★ (☝☝▮▣✕). The ruins of the ancient town lie in an extraordinary position high above the Tyrrhenian Sea. The best view down to the lagoon of Oliveri is from the pilgrimage church. The marvellous beaches are reached from Oliveri (▲△✕), where an environmental protection group, Lega Ambiente, has signposted a short walk. The little hotel Quattro Stagioni, in the neighbouring town of Falcone (▲✕) has excellent cooking.

From Castroreale Terme the SS185 takes you inland through

beautiful landscapes, with the now-familiar Peloritani Mountains to the east and the gentler Nebrodi range (Car tour 3) to the west. While the road winds uphill, you look back over the coast and the Aeolian Islands. **Novara di Sicilia★** (110km 𝑖🕭✕💺📻) is an inviting small town, so far almost untouched by tourism. It's a good place to shop for a picnic.

Climbing further towards the Portella Mandrazzi, the SS185 runs through light deciduous woods at the foot of the Rocca Novara. The crossroads at the **Bivio Fondacheli** (117km; Picnic 4; Walk 14) is the starting point for the climb to the Rocca Novara. Soon you reach the **Portella Mandrazzi** (119km), the watershed between the Tyrrhenian and Ionian seas. Now the road descends in deep hairpin bends to the Alcantara Valley, with an excellent panorama towards Mount Etna. Ignoring the turn-off to Francavilla (126km), drive on to a crossroads (136km), where the road continues towards Randazzo in the west. *Now* turn left towards Francavilla and, at the next crossroads (139km), go right towards Castiglione di Sicilia, soon crossing a bridge over the Alcantara (Picnic 5). **Castiglione di Sicilia★** (143km 🕭🛏🏠📷✕💺) is a medieval small town strikingly poised above the Alcantara Valley. From its castle rock you would enjoy a most beautiful view of Mount Etna and the mountains in northern Sicily.

Beyond some vineyards you come into **Linguaglossa★** (152km 𝑖🕭🛏✕💺M). This pretty town is a starting point for excursions on the northern slopes of Etna (Car tour 1; Walks 4-7). Linguaglossa and Piedimonte Etneo are also good places to shop for a picnic.

From **Piedimonte Etneo** to **Fiumefreddo di Sicila** (163km) the SS120 runs through a neatly-cultivated landscape, with views to Taormina, Castelmola and Monte Venere (Walk 9). Before returning to Taormina, make a short excursion to the sea. Follow the Strada Provinciale towards Marina di Cottone, past the **Castello degli Schiavi**. A few hundred metres before the beach, on the left, you pass the entrance to the Riserva del Fiumefreddo. In the Visitors' Centre (open from 08.30-16.30 in autumn and winter, 09.00-18.00 spring and summer) you can pick up a plan of this nature reserve — a fine place for a short ramble, past springs surrounded by reeds, high horse-tails and papyrus. The only other place in Sicily where you'll see papyrus is along the Ciane (Walk 36). After perhaps having a swim on the fine-pebble beach of **Marina di Cottone** (165km; Picnic 6) return via **Giardini Naxos** (173km 𝑖🍴📷🛏△✕💺M) to **Taormina** (177km).

Lipari: kaolin mines at Quattropani (Walk 13)

Car tour 3: THE NEBRODI MOUNTAINS

S. Fratello • Portella Femmina Morta • Cesarò • Castello Maniace • Randazzo • Floresta • Galati Mamertino • Alcara li Fusi • Sant'Agata di Militello

165km/102mi; 5-6 hours' driving

On route: Picnics (see pages 9-14) 7-9; Walks 15-18 (with accommodation tips)

With the exception of the narrow and poorly-asphalted road between Tortorici and Alcara li Fusi, most of the roads are good. Alcara li Fusi can also be easily reached directly from Sant'Agata di Militello. The Nebrodi are extensively wooded, and so are rich in water, with frequent fountains along the road. It's a good idea to break up this tour into at least two days.

This tour runs through Sicily's most densely-wooded area, the Parco Regionale dei Nebrodi, a protected nature reserve since 1993. Lying between the Peloritani Mountains in the east (Car tour 2) and the Madonie in the west (Car tour 4), the Nebrodi rise parallel with the island's north coast. The main crest, largely wooded in beech, reaches its highest elevation at Monte Soro (1847m/6058ft). Animal husbandry is widespread in these mountains and, whether you're driving or out walking, you'll frequently meet herds of cattle, sheep, horses and pigs. Try the local cuisine in one of the inconspicuous roadside restaurants *(baracche)*.

From the **km125 road-marker** on the **SS113** (between Acquedolci and the motorway exit Sant'Agata di Militello), take the SS289 towards Cesarò. The road climbs in hairpin bends up into the foothills of the Nebrodi. On the ascent you look back over the coastal plain, Capo d'Orlando and the Aeolian Islands in the east, and Cefalù in the west. The road skirts Monte San Fratello and reaches San Fratello's cemetery (12km).

The SS289 runs through **San Fratello** (♗▲✕) and climbs to a ridge between the valleys of the Fiume Rosmarino and the Torrente San Fratello. You cross several vegetational zones, from woods of turkey oak to holm oak and finally beech, before you reach the **Portella Femmina Morta** (34km; Picnic 7; Walk 15). At 1524m/ 4999ft, this is the highest pass in the Nebrodi.

From the Portella Femmina Morta the SS289 descends towards the south, after 500m passing the **Villa Miraglia**, surrounded by beech woods. During the summer you might see charcoal burners at work along the road. At the Piano Cicogna you come into the oak zone once again. Then the woods thin out and give way to grazing areas. Views open out inland: the village of Troina rises on a rock in the west, like an eagle's nest, while the silhouette of Mount Etna closes off the eastern horizon.

In **Cesarò** (50km *i*▲✕🖵📷; Picnic 8) follow the signposts 'Bivio SS120' until you meet the SS120. Turn left here, towards Randazzo, with Etna straight ahead of you. Shortly after crossing the Simeto River, where a road goes right towards Bronte, there are some good restaurants near the crossroads.

Continuing on the SS120, turn left (65km) for Maniace, to take

Maniace — Castello Nelson (Picnic 9)

a worthwhile little detour. It's only 2.5km to the **Castello Maniace★** (♨♁弄✿Mwc; Picnic 9). This former abbey lies on the shore of the Torrente Saracena. Apart from the 12th-century Norman church, you can visit the manor house (now called Castello Nelson) and the beautifully-landscaped park. In gratitude for Nelson's help in fleeing Naples on board his flagship during the Napoleonic invasion, the Bourbon King Ferdinand IV gave Admiral Nelson the Dukedom of Bronte and the Castello Maniace, together with the extensive estates which today bear his name.

Return to the SS120 (70km) and continue towards Randazzo. Coming into the western side of **Randazzo★** (84km ♨♁∎✿▲✕ ☻M), turn left on a cobbled street towards the *'centro storico'*. Park after a few hundred metres, in front of the Porta S. Martino, and then stroll into the old town on foot. Despite heavy bombardments and destruction during the Second World War, a medieval atmosphere still prevails in the old town. The castle and the three main churches tower above a sea of low buildings.

Continuing the tour on the SS120, you drive around the old town before turning left on the SS116 towards Santa Domenica Vittoria and Floresta. A bridge takes you over the Alcantara River. Look back and you'll see Etna rising majestically behind the town of Randazzo. Natural hazards can be an everyday occurrence in some parts of Sicily: the SS116 had to be rebuilt after a landslide. The road climbs quickly up to **Santa Domenica Vittoria** (✕), then rises quite gently through light oak woods. A number of picnic sites line the road (☗). Shortly before Floresta, a wide basin opens out, collecting the headwaters of the Alcantara. **Floresta** (97km ✕), at 1260m/4133ft, is the highest village in Sicily. You can buy excellent cheese in the grocer's shops.

The SS116 descends from Floresta towards Capo d'Orlando, but after 7.5km (105km), turn left and follow the narrow secondary road towards Tortorici. The road snakes downhill to **Tortorici** (120km 🛉✕🖵) and then rises again to **Galati Mamertino★** (135km 🛉✕🖵). There are many art treasures in the churches in this village, where Walk 16 begins and ends (on the southern outskirts).

From the western outskirts of Galati Mamertino keep straight ahead, following signposting for the 'Trattoria Portella Gazzana' (where a right turn leads to the Agriturismo Margherita). You can see Longi across the valley, with the rocks of the Roche del Crasto rising behind it. The road descends in the valley, where you cross a bridge and then turn left, still following signposting for the 'Trattoria Portella Gazzana'. At the next crossroads, turn right uphill, until you reach a wider crossroads with a watering place. Turn left here, soon reaching the **Portella Gazzana** (145km ✕; Walks 17 and 18).

Turn right just beyond the Trattoria Portella Gazzana. This narrow road leads to **Alcara li Fusi★** (150km 🛉🏔✕🖵). At the southern entrance to the village you'll find the lovely fountain shown below, the Fontana Abate. One of the offices of the Parco dei Nebrodi is located in the village.

With marvellous views across the valley to San Marco d'Alunzio★ (🛉🏔M), the SP161 now takes you through **Militello Rosmarino★** and back down to the coastal SS113. Turn left here, to **Sant' Agata di Militello** (165km 🏔🖵M).

*Alcara li Fusi —
the Fontana Abate*

Car tour 4: CEFALÙ AND THE MADONIE MOUNTAINS

Cefalù • Gibilmanna • Castelbuono • Geraci Siculo • Gangi •
Petralia Soprana • Petralia Sottana • Polizzi Generosa • Piano
Battaglia • Isnello • Cefalù

161km/100mi; 5-6 hours' driving

En route: Picnics (see pages 9-14) 10-12; Walks 19-23 (with accommodation
tips)

*Most of the roads in the Madonie Mountains are in good condition. Except for
the weekends, there is little traffic. Piano Zucchi and Piano Battaglia are popular
winter sports areas, so the roads are cleared of snow in winter. This tour could
also be started on the PA-CT motorway, by taking the 'Tre Monzelli' exit. The
SS120 via Gangi, Sperlinga, Nicosia and Troina to Cesarò is an especially scenic
stretch — Etna is in front of you the whole way. Using this road you could link
up this car tour with Car tour 3.*

Cefalù is a place where you can really feel at home. The clean,
stone-cobbled streets are ideal for strolling, and the long sandy
beach is ideal for swimming. But it is the mighty Norman cathedral
and the defiant castle rock that give this medieval town its
unmistakable face. This tour sets out from Cefalù to explore the
Madonie Mountains, a unique cultural and natural landscape that
has been protected as the Parco delle Madonie since 1989. A
number of pretty villages form a wreath around the Madonie. The
Pizzo Carbonara, at 1979m/6491ft, is Sicily's second highest peak.
The Madonie are characterised by extensive limestone areas, and
woods with the largest number of species in the Mediterranean. On
the walks you will come upon botanic rarities like the giant hollies
(Ilex aquifolium) at the Piano Pomo and the Nebrodi firs *(Abies
nebrodensis)* in the Vallone Madonna degli Angeli — both relics
of the Tertiary Era, which are otherwise extinct. Sheep-breeding still
is of great economic importance here, and an excellent cheese is
produced in the Madonie.

From **Cefalù★** (*†ⓘⓣⅢ▦⌨▲✕🚆⊕M*; Picnic 10; Walk 19) follow
signposting for Gibilmanna, heading inland. The well-built road
rises past olive groves, with marvellous views back to Cefalù's
castle rock and the sea. After several kilometres Pizzo S. Angelo
with its observatory appears ahead. To the right you can see the
narrow mountain chain separating Gratteri from Isnello. At this
height you'll encounter the first manna ashes *(Fraxinus ornus)*; the
latex from these trees *(manna)* has been extracted by the local
people for centuries and is used as a sweetening substance and for
medical purposes. Turn left on the short cul-de-sac road branching
off to the **Santuario Maria SS di Gibilmanna** (15km *†M*; Picnic 11).
The monastery/convent lies on the western slope of Pizzo S. Angelo
in the midst of oak woods, an inviting place to take a break.

Leaving the sanctuary, continue south. Beyond the pass (16km)
keep straight ahead towards Castelbuono. With a view towards the
central Madonie massif, the road leads into a bucolic valley
landscape, where the pretty town of Isnello lies at the foot of Pizzo
Dipillo. A bridge takes you across the valley's ravine and, shortly

after, you turn left on the SP9 towards Castelbuono (23km). In the west the village of Pollina is visible atop a cone-shaped mountain. Just a little later Castelbuono also comes into sight, with the defiant castle for which the town was named. Take the bypass circling to the north of the town (33km), and park just below the castle; from here it's just a short way into the old town of **Castelbuono★** (*i†▮▲✕🅿M*).

Leaving Castelbuono, turn right on the SS286 towards Geraci Siculo. Just before you reach the southern boundary of Castelbuono (35km), a cul-de-sac branches off to the right, leading up to the Piano Sempria (22km return; *▲▮✕*; Walk 20). After leaving Castelbuono behind, the road leads through a rolling landscape covered with orchards and olive groves. A dramatic view opens up to Pizzo Canna and Monte Ferro in the west. The road ascends past oak woods and cork oak groves *(Quercus suber)*. The SS286 circles to the west of **Geraci Siculo★** (56km *i†▮🖼▲▲✕🅿M*). A splendid fountain lies at the southern boundary of the village, just below the castle; Geraci's mineral water is well-known and is bottled.

From Geraci the road descends again, and at the **Bivio Geraci** you meet the crossing SS120 (62km). Turn left here, to **Gangi★** (70km *i†▲▲✕🅿🖼*; Walk 23): this short detour is worthwhile, if only to view the town from a distance.

From Gangi turn back along the SS120, towards Petralia Soprana. After some 5km, leave the SS120 (which bypasses Petralia Soprana to the south) and turn right on the SP29 (83km), to make a short visit to this pretty town. Driving up to Petralia Soprana you notice its tight medieval cluster straight away. You can park in the Piazza del Popolo, right in the centre of **Petralia Soprana★** (87km *i†▲✕🖼M*). The town has many art treasures, and some of the churches are very old. The Chiesa Madre, dedicated to the patron saints SS. Pietro e Paolo, dates back to the 9th century. From the Piazza del Popolo the Via del Loreto leads past the church of the same name to the Belvedere 'U Castru' (Picnic 12).

Gangi

Cefalù and the Norman cathedral

From Petralia Soprana the road descends to **Petralia Sottana**★ (90km 🚶🍴✕🚌🚐M). The excellent hotel Albergo Madonie and the administrative offices of the Parco delle Madonie are both on the Corso Paolo Agliata.

From Petralia Sottana take the SS120 again, now making for Polizzi Generosa. (Another scenic road goes from Petralia to the Portella Colla via the Piano Battaglia.) Gently-sloping hills, fields, pastures and olive groves accompany you to **Castellana Sicula** (84km 🚶🍴🏔🏔✕🚌M). Then the road ascends gently again and you turn right on the SS643 towards Polizzi Generosa (102km.) The small houses of **Polizzi Generosa**★ (90km 🚶🍴🏔🏔✕🚌🚐M) huddle on an mountain buttress. The origins of Polizzi are ancient; the town reached its acme during the Norman period. Without entering the centre, head right towards Collesano on the SP119, driving under an old aqueduct. Soon the 'amphitheatre' of the Quacella Mountains rises in front of you, opening out to the west. After the km8 road-marker (114km), you pass the starting point for Walk 21 (by the green iron gate of the forestry commission). The Cervi massif rises in front of you, and you reach the **Portella Colla** (117km). The road branching off to the right here leads to the Piano Battaglia (🏔; Walk 22), while the forestry road on the left makes a pleasant walk to the Piano Cervi.

Continue along the Vallone Madonie towards Piano Zucchi (🏔). The roads descends in hairpins, with the rock walls of the Carbonara massif rising high on the right (Walk 22). Alpine pastures alternate with beautiful forests. In the west you can see Monte S. Calogero (Walk 35) and the gulf of Termini Imerese. You pass a road on the left to Collesano (131km; it's the fastest route to the Palermo/Cefalù motorway). Keep right here, to **Isnello**★ (138km 🚶🏔🏔✕🚌). Not far past the town, turn left towards Gibilmanna (139km) and retrace your outward route back to **Cefalù** (161km).

Car tour 5: PALERMO AND WESTERN SICILY

Palermo • Monreale • Segesta • Scopello • Erice • Trapani • Marsala • Selinunte • S. Giuseppe Iato • Palermo

250km/155mi; 7-8 hours' driving

En route: Picnics (see pages 9-14) 13-16; Walks 24-29 (with accommodation tips)

This tour to the western part of Sicily mainly follows secondary roads and only occasionally uses the motorway or national roads. Scopello, Erice, Trapani (if you want to get out to the Egadi Islands), and Marinella di Selinunte are good places to break the tour with an overnight stay.

Modern-day Palermo is one of the most interesting cities in Italy. You can stroll for days in the Arabian-style maze of streets in the old town and discover oriental markets, hot food stalls, typical trattorias, medieval churches built by the Norman rulers, baroque palaces, Art Nouveau architecture, parks with gigantic ficus trees and wonderful museums. The only thing you need forego in Palermo is driving a car.

In western Sicily you not only approach North Africa geographically but, in the midst of extensive vineyards surrounded by date palms, you come upon the *bagli*, fortified estates typical of the region. The villages are frequently reminiscent of Arabian kasbahs. The influence of the Arabs never completely disappeared after their expulsion in the Middle Ages. One of the typical Trapanese dishes on all the menus is *cuscusu*. And couscous wasn't brought to Sicily by recent immigrants from Tunisia, their ancestors had already taken care of that a long time ago. On this tour you will not only get to know some of Sicily's most beautiful archaeological sites, but a visit to the island of Levanzo gives you a glimpse of the Stone Age. One of Sicily's most beautiful coastlines is en route as well — the Parco dello Zingaro, a protected nature reserve.

Follow the Corso Vittorio Emanuele out of the centre of **Palermo★** (♟♦♥▲✕▤⊕❀M; Picnic 13; Walk 24), past the cathedral and Palazzo dei Normanni. At the Piazza Indipendenza turn half-right into Via Capuccini, with the prominent peak of Monte Cuccio ahead. Cross the ring road and, in **Boccadifalco**, follow the signposts straight ahead to 'San Martino delle Scale' and 'Abbazia Benedettina'. Only few kilometres after leaving Palermo behind, you are surrounded by an impressive mountain panorama. In **San Martino delle Scale★** (12km ♦✕▱▤) follow the road to the left, past the Benedictine abbey. The Gulf of Palermo opens up now, and Pizzo del Corvo rises in front of you, crowned by its castle (Walk 25). An official picnic site, offering marvellous views (Picnic 14; photograph page 11) lies on the hill to the right of the road. At the next junction (13km), turn left, following signs for 'Castellaccio' and 'Monreale'. The starting point for Walk 25 lies just on the saddle at the foot of Pizzo del Corvo (14km). The semicircular mountain range enclosing Palermo and the Conca d'Oro unfolds in front of you now, with Monte Pellegrino (Walk 24) edging the western side of the Conca d'Oro. Below lies the cathedral of Monreale with its famous cloister. To visit **Monreale★** (20km i✝☗📷✕⛽❀), turn left at the crossroads at the southern edge of the village. Then continue on the SP69 towards Partinico.

Drive through **Pioppo** and, at the following crossroads (28km), turn right on the SS186, still following the signpost 'Partinico'. A wild and lonely mountain landscape surrounds you. Soon a fantastic view opens out to the Gulf of Castellamare and the mountains of the Parco dello Zingaro (Walk 27). The road leads above Borgetto and Partinico, where the extensive vineyards of western Sicily begin (the local Bianco d'Alcamo, for example, is an excellent white DOC wine).

At the roundabout southwest of **Partinico** (51km) take the SS113 towards Trapani. You can already see the town of Alcamo at the foot of Monte Bonifato. In **Alcamo★** (i✝♜✕⛽) continue on the SS113, now following a particularly scenic stretch of road. Not far past Calatafimi's railway station, turn right (71km), following the brown signposts for 'Segesta'. The narrow road circles to the east of Monte Barbaro and leads straight to the archaeological site of **Segesta★** (74km Π✕⛩📷WC). Plan enough time for your visit — the unfinished, but still standing temple is a unique building. Climbing Monte Pispisa offers you an bird's-eye view of it. A footpath within the archaeological area itself leads up to the ancient theatre on Monte Barbaro.

Secondary roads now take you to Castellamare del Golfo. Drive past the motorway exit and Segesta's railway station, then go under the motorway. Just afterwards, turn right, crossing the railway, towards Castellamare (76km). Driving east through a hilly and agricultural landscape, you pass the **Terme Segestane** (82km). These hot springs have been famous since antiquity; one can still swim in the little modern public swimming baths until 23.00. At the edge of **Castellamare** (89km i✝♜▲▲△✕⛽), turn left at the traffic lights and follow the SS187 towards Trapani, overlooking the picturesque port of Castellamare. After a few kilometres turn right on a cul-de-sac road (94km) towards Scopello. **Scopello★** (99km i▲▲✕📷; photograph page 8) has some pleasant hotels and a couple of good restaurants. The Parco dello Zingaro, a nature reserve not far north of Scopello, is perfect for hiking and swimming (Picnic 15; Walk 27; photograph page 107).

Back on the SS187 (104km) drive towards Trapani. The scattered fortified estates *(bagli)* are typical of this area. Erice dominates the rock plateau rising in the west. Shortly after the km18 road-marker on the SS187, turn right towards Custonaci and S. Vito lo Capo (120km), with the peak of Monte Còfano rising ahead. On meeting a crossroads at the western edge of Custonaci (123km), turn left towards Trapani. (The road to the right leads to S. Vito lo Capo (i▲▲△✕📷), a seaside resort with beautiful sandy beaches and many hotels.)

Leave the Trapani road (127km), turning right towards 'Grotta Mangiapane', a rewarding diversion. Following the brown signposts (the last stretch along a gravel road), you reach the **Grotta Mangiapane**★ (130km; Walk 26) and may be surprised to find a tiny, but perfectly-formed village inside this cave! Today this small *borgo* lies deserted and only comes to life during its Christmas nativity play.

Continue the tour by following the coast, then turn off left for Erice (137km); the coastal road continues past the Tonnara di Bonagia (▲▲✕) to Trapani. This very scenic road leads inland past **Valderice** (▲▲△) and up to **Erice**★ (149km *i̇✝*▦▲▲✕🖼❀M). The small medieval town, a very popular shrine to Aphrodite in antiquity, is a much-visited tourist attraction today. You can stroll for hours on the cobbled streets, enjoying splendid views. From up here you look down on Trapani, the glistening salt-flats and the Egadi Islands. Erice is also well known for its almond pastries.

The continuing road leads down the western slope of Monte Erice to Trapani. A sea of white houses covers the crescent-shaped peninsula, and the Egadi Islands lie off the coast. In **Trapani**★ (155km *i̇✝*▲▲✕🖳⊕🖼M) head west on the four-lane Via Fardella. Beyond the municipal park, follow Via Garibaldi past elegant baroque palaces. Always keeping in the same direction, you reach the promontory at the Torre di Ligny (160km 🖼M). The coastal road runs south past the port (162km), from where ships sail to the Egadi Islands (Walk 28). Following the brown signposts 'Riserva Naturale delle Saline' and 'Isola di Mozia', drive through the industrial suburbs, then continue towards Marsala. You will pass a cul-de-sac road off right to the 'Museo delle Saline' in Nubia (+5km return). The fascinating age-old landscape of the salt flats stretches along the coast from Trapani to Marsala. Some kilometres beyond the village of **Marausa**, turn left on the SP21 (179km). Again following brown signposts (for 'Isola di Mozia' and 'Riserva Naturale Isole dello Stagnone') you reach the **Imbarcadero di Mozia** (186km; photograph page 15), from where boats sail to the island of Mozia. Mozia (also called S. Pantaleone) floats in the midst of Sicily's largest lagoon. The island was an important Punic colony called Mozia. The excavations and the little museum on Mozia★ (**𝝅**🖼Mᴡᴄ; Picnic 16) are certainly worth a visit.

The west coast road takes you to **Marsala**★ (*i̇✝𝝅*▲▲✕🖳⊕M), where you follow signs for the 'Museo Archeologico-Nave Punica'. The archaeological museum is housed in the Baglio Anselmi (196km). In front of the Baglio Florio (199km), one of the world-famous wine cellars, turn right on the SS115 and head out of town, making for Mazara del Vallo. At **Campobello di Mazara** leave the SS115 (218km) and drive along the western edge of the village towards 'Tre Fontane', soon turning right to the 'Cave di Cusa'. The road ends at a gravel parking place (221km). The **Cave di Cusa**★ (**𝝅**; Picnic 17; photograph page 10, top left), one of the ancient quarries of Selinunte, gives you an interesting insight into the civil engineering skills of the ancient Greeks.

Skirt to the south of Campobello di Mazara and follow the SP60 towards Menfi. The narrow road crosses the Modione Valley. Across the vineyards to your right you can see the acropolis of ancient Selinunte, with the sea as a backdrop. Following signs to Selinunte, turn right and, after a few kilometres, you reach the entrance to the archaeological zone of **Selinunte★** (236km *i***ℿ**WC), one of the largest in Europe. Nowhere else in Sicily better brings to life the times of the ancient Greeks. The nearby seaside resort of **Marinella di Selinunte** (**▲✕**) stretches along a beautiful sandy beach.

From Marinella continue towards Castelvetrano (**M**) and follow the motorway a short distance towards Palermo. Turn off at the **Salemi exit** (160km) to **Gibellina Nuova**. Together with 13 other villages, Gibellina was destroyed in a devastating earthquake in 1968. After many years, which the surviving citizens had to spend in portacabins, the town was rebuilt in a new location. Although well-known architects and numerous artists have participated in the design, the result is strongly controversial and is regarded by some as the second catastrophe — this one man-made. Follow the signposts 'Ruderi di Gibellina'. This narrow winding road leads past **S. Ninfa**, and through a neatly-cultivated landscape. Wine is the main crop. The wide Belice Valley opens up ahead, and mountains rise to the east. From far away one can already see the huge concrete sculpture by Alberto Burri, which covers the ruins of Gibellina like a shroud. Turn right towards Poggioreale and Salaparuta (178km), passing the roadside ruins of devastated buildings. A narrow cul-de-sac road heads left up to the **Ruderi** (Ruins) **di Gibellina★** (180km).

The road continues past the ruins of old Salaparuta (where the signposting is somewhat confusing). Go through modern **Salaparuta** (186km) and continue towards the Sciacca/Palermo highway. This wide road, the SS624, will take you back to Palermo. Beyond Roccamena, the rocks of the Rocca Busambra (Walk 31) rise steeply in the east. Monte Iato, with S. Cipirello spread at its feet, takes shape in front of you. To reach the archaeological site on Monte Iato, take the 'S. Cipirello, Partinico' exit (221km), then follow signs for 'Antica Iato'. To reach Piana degli Albanesi (Walk 29) take the eponymous exit further on and follow the SP34.

The SS624 circles to the west of **S. Cipirello** (*i***✕🚮M**) and **S. Giuseppe Iato** (**ℿ▲✕🚮🖃**). This part of the expressway was only completed after an influential mafia clan was broken up at the beginning of the 1990s (giving rise to its name: Strada della Liberazione). The road cuts through a mountain range and the Conca d'Oro suddenly fills the windscreen again. If you would like to visit Monreale now, take the Giacalone exit (231km); otherwise follow the SS624 through the Oreto Valley back to **Palermo** (250km).

Car tour 6: BETWEEN PALERMO AND AGRIGENTO

Palermo • Piana degli Albanesi • Ficuzza • Corleone • Prizzi • Palazzo Adriano • Caltabelotta • Sciacca • Eraclea Minoa • Agrigento • Sant'Angelo Muxaro • Cammarata • Caccamo • Solunto • Palermo

448km/277mi; 10 hours' driving

En route: Picnics (see pages 9-14) 18-20; Walks 24, 29-35 (with accommodation tips)

Good, but not overly-busy secondary roads take you on this tour through central Sicily. Even though the marvellous landscapes you see along the route are not frequented by tourists, you won't have any problem finding good places to stay overnight.

Palermo and Agrigento are without doubt high on the list of priorities during any trip to Sicily. But the inland region behind these two provincial capitals remains undiscovered by most visitors. Only a few kilometres south of Palermo there's a mountain region reminiscent of the Alps. Even the local people knew little about it, until Palermo's tourist board created and mapped out a network of marked hiking trails in the late 1990s. (Unfortunately tourist boards change, and so do their priorities: the trails are no longer maintained. Alas, this is also true for Walk 29.) Piana degli Albanesi is one of the inland villages en route: Albanians settled here in the 15th century and have kept their language and Greek Orthodox customs throughout the centuries. Names like Corleone and Prizzi, thanks to the movies, allude to more sinister things! Have a look for yourself and visit these towns, which are trying to overcome their 'mafia' image. Connoisseurs agree: Caltabelotta is one of Sicily's most beautiful villages. Weathered gypsum hills, strangely shaped, characterise the province of Agrigento. The Monti Sicani range was declared a regional nature reserve in 2012.

From the southern ring road at **Palermo★** (♦✝⚄▲✕🖫⊕❀M; Picnic 13; Walk 24) head south on the SS624 towards Sciacca. You approach the mountain chain on the southern side of the Conca d'Oro. To the right lies Monreale★. At the Altofonte exit (5km) turn off towards Piana degli Albanesi. The road (SP5) squeezes through **Altofonte** (9km), then leads from an austere mountain landscape with hardly any trees up to a well-cultivated plateau. At a junction (30km) turn right towards Piana degli Albanesi. On the road signs the village is announced in two languages, Albanian and Italian. The Greek Orthodox cathedral of **Piana degli Albanesi★** stands right in the main square (33km ✝▲✕🖫). Signs here also show the way to hiking trails on the Pizzuta peak west of Piana (Walk 29).

Drive down the Corso and continue along the SP5 towards Ficuzza and Corleone. You pass Piana's large reservoir, which supplies Palermo with drinking water. After a short rise, the road descends southeast, and the Rocca Busambra starts to appear. The Bosco della Ficuzza, Sicily's largest single oak forest, stretches out to the north: once a royal hunting ground, it is today a protected nature reserve. When you meet the SS118 (51km), turn right towards

32

Ficuzza and Corleone. Shortly afterwards, at an obelisk (52km), turn left to the hunting palace of **Ficuzza★** (53.5km ⬗✕⛱☀M; Picnic 18). Beyond Ficuzza the road (later unsurfaced) continues to the Rifugio Alpe Cucco, a mountain inn (⛰✕; Walks 30 and 31).

Return to the SS118 and continue towards Corleone. Views of the Rocca Busambra accompany you to the left. The road skirts the eastern side of **Corleone** (71km *i*⛰⬤✕⊟) and continues towards Prizzi and Agrigento. To the right lies the old town of Corleone, partly hidden in a narrow canyon. Turn left to make a short, but recommended, detour into **Prizzi★** (95km ⛄⬤⛒), a small town spread along a plateau. Returning from Prizzi, meet the SS188 and turn right towards Palazzo Adriano (99km). The wide Sosio Valley opens out in front of you while the road gently descends, finally coming into **Palazzo Adriano★** (109km *i*⛄⬤✕⊟; Walk 32). This pretty village was the setting for the Oscar-winning film *Cinema Paradiso* in 1989. The village is as delightful in reality as it was in the film, but few visitors find their way here. Now they are trying to attract nature-lovers, who can enjoy some fantastic walks in the Sosio Valley and surrounding mountains.

After Palazzo Adriano the SS188 crosses to the northern side of the Sosio Valley and climbs in hairpins. While you'll not find a lot of traffic on the road, in spring you *will* come upon huge flocks of sheep. The small mountain village of Giuliana can be seen in the distance. The road leads south through **Chiusa Sclafani** (127km) and continues towards Burgio. Eventually the jagged mountaintops of Caltabelotta appear. At the edge of **S. Carlo** (137km), turn right on the SP19 towards Caltabelotta. While this narrow and poorly-asphalted road rapidly gains height, you can look down on Ribera and the coastal plain. When you get to the roundabout in **Caltabelotta★** (122km ⛄*i*▥⛒✕⊟; Picnic 19), follow the sign 'centro' uphill to the right. There is a large car park below the Chiesa Matrice (123km). Without doubt the medieval centre and the marvellous views amply compensate for the winding mountain road.

From Caltabelotta take the SP37 down towards Sciacca. On a clear day not only wide stretches of the coast lie spread out at your feet, but you might even get a glimpse of the Pelagie Islands and Pantelleria. On the outskirts of **Sciacca★** (143km *i*⛄⬤✕⊟⊕M), turn left on the SS115 towards Agrigento. Sciacca, with its large fishing port, spas and many ceramic shops, is well worth a short stop. The old town is best approached from the east: from the SS115 follow the signs into the centre (150km).

Back on the SS115 you cross the Platani River; its estuary is a protected nature reserve. Shortly after the bridge (170km), turn right on a cul-de-sac road to the archaeological site of **Eraclea Minoa★** (175km ▥⛒Mwc) — and one of Sicily's best sandy beaches at the **Capo Bianco★** (177km ⬗✕⛒; Picnic 20).

The SS115 continues through a landscape of rugged and barren gypsum hills, their slopes glittering bizarrely in the sun. Past **Monte-allegro** (Walk 33) and **Siciliana** (♠︎✕🍽︎) you reach **Porto Empe-docle** (208km). The industrial harbour town of Agrigento is the birthplace of the bestselling author Andrea Cammileri. Drive round the south side of Agrigento, following the signs 'Caltanissetta' and 'Casa Pirandello' (the house where this Nobel Prize winner was born can be visited). To the left you can see the new town of Agrigento and, in the foreground, the ancient temples splendidly aligned along a ridge. They are listed among the UNESCO World Heritage Sites. Turn off at the exit for 'Agrigento, S. Leone' (216km) and drive towards the temples and the town. After the roundabout you reach a large car park just in front of the temples (218km *i*🍴☕wc). The temples are best visited early in the morning or late in the afternoon, when the light is better for photography and there are fewer tourists. If you follow the road uphill, past the Hotel Villa Athena, the archaeological museum, and the excavations of a Roman quarter, you will come to the Piazza Marconi in modern **Agrigento★** (223km *i*🍴📷🏔︎✕🍽︎⊕M).

Follow the signs 'Palermo', to leave from the north side of Agrigento, quickly passing modern housing and industrial estates and returning to a rural landscape. Leave the SS189 at the 'Aragona' exit (235km) and drive to **Aragona** (237km). In the village yellow signs show the way to the 'Vulcanelli di Macalube'. About 3km south of the village, in the midst of fields, you come across a strange lunar landscape, where escaping methane gases left small mud volcanoes behind. Continue on the badly-asphalted road past **S. Elisabetta**, making for Sant'Angelo Muxaro. The winding route leads through a landscape of glittering gypsum hills. The Camma-

Siciliana, with Chrysanthemum segetum *in the foreground*

rata Mountains rise in the north. Sant'Angelo lies just ahead of you on a plateau; several cave openings (Bronze Age tombs) are visible on the southern slope. An access road takes you up to **Sant'Angelo Muxaro★** (258km 🚶🏕🍴🏔✕🏨; Walk 34). Despite no famous buildings to boast, Sant'Angelo makes a very attractive first impression. Giuseppe Tirrito, the former young mayor, promoted the real resources of his commune: a beautiful landscape, an interesting gypsum cave, the Bronze Age tombs and, most importantly, the natural hospitality of its people. The old mule tracks have been refurbished and offer good walking possibilities.

A bridge takes you across the Platani River and then the road ascends rapidly in hairpins to **S. Biagio Platani** (265km). Pastures, occasionally interrupted by olive, almond and peach groves, cover the rolling hills. The rural landscape is dominated by the heavily-wooded Monti Cammarata in the north. Steadily climbing, the road takes you through **Alessandria della Rocca** (253km) and then along the SS118 to **Bivona** (290km). Bivona has a nice old centre and is a good place for a short stop (you could shop for a picnic). In **Santo Stefano Quisquina** (298km) turn off right towards Cammarata. The SP24 is narrow and badly-asphalted in places. The surrounding landscape on the other hand is superb. When you reach a pass (300km), turn left up a cul-de-sac road to the **Eremo della Quisquina** (301.5km 🚶🏨). The view is breathtaking! Legend has it that S. Rosalia lived here as an hermit before she moved on to a cave on Monte Pellegrino near Palermo (Walk 24).

Continue the tour along the northern slopes of the Cammarata Mountains, enjoying the views over to the Madonie and Mount Etna. The forestry commission has set up a number of picnic areas along the road (🌲). A few kilometres before you get to the village of Cammarata, turn right up another cul-de-sac and climb to the antennas on the top of Monte Cammarata (324km). After about 2.5km you reach the Primo Rifugio (✕), from where a hiking trail ascends to the Bivio Romeo and a forestry road continues to Monte Gemini (8km/5mi; 3h30min).

At the western edge of **Cammarata** (326km 🏔✕🏨) you pass the simple Hotel Falco Azzuro. The neighbouring village of **San Giovanni Gemini** runs seamlessly along from Cammarata. The way through this village is a little confusing: follow the signs 'AG-PA' until you reach the SS189 (335km), then head north towards Palermo, following the upper valley of the Platani. The SS189 has been widened into an expressway and is the main trunk road between Palermo and Agrigento. The hillsides sloping gently to the south alternate between pastures and fields of grain. Past **Lercara Friddi**, birthplace of the mafia gangster Lucky Luciano, you reach the SS121 (360km). Leave the SS189 here, turing right on the SS285 to **Roccapalumba** (364km 🏔✕). Past the Hotel La Rocca, you drive through the small village spread at the foot of a huge rock. The route via **Regalgioffoli** to Caccamo is especially scenic, with the imposing ridges of the Serra della Cimina and the Rocca Busambra (Walk 31) rising in the west and the Madonie to the east. With views towards Monte S. Calogero (Walk 35), you come into **Caccamo★** (390km ♦♦♦♦✕♦♦), dominated by the mighty castle of the Chiaramonte. From the junction at the southern edge of the town, turn left into the old centre (the road to the right leads to Walk 35).

From Caccamo the SS285 descends towards the sea. Monte S. Calogero rises to the right, and Cefalù with the Madonie appear once more. Shortly before Termini Imerese (400km) you can decide whether to shorten the tour by returning to Palermo on the motorway. In **Termini Imerese★** (401km ♦♦♦♦♦✕♦♦♦), which is a much nicer town than the port and industries lead you to believe, follow the signs 'Ponte S. Leonardo' and 'SS 113'. A baroque bridge takes you over the Fiume S. Leonardo (404km). Drive along the coast, with fine views to Capo Zafferana. The old tuna factory in **Trabia** (♦♦✕) has been transformed into the pleasant Hotel Tonnara di Trabia. In **Casteldaccia** (410km) drive straight on towards Solunto and, shortly before the S. Flavia railway station, turn right towards 'Porticello' and 'Solunto' (413km). At the next crossing, after about 500m, keep straight ahead on a cul-de-sac road up to the archaeological site of **Solunto★** (445km ♦♦wc). Ancient Solunto has a beautiful mountainside setting with far-reaching views.

Continue driving along the coast. The charming fishing port of **Porticello** (✕) is famous for its good restaurants. After circling Capo Zafferana and Capo Mongerbino, the view west opens up to the Gulf of Palermo, Palermo itself and Monte Pellegrino (Walk 24). Before Aspra, turn left (433km) to **Bagheria★** (434km ♦♦♦♦M), where the Palermitan nobility built splendid baroque villas in the 17th and 18th centuries, to escape the oppressive summer heat of the capital. The post-war building boom invaded these lush parks with faceless apartment blocks. The most famous of the villas, the Villa Palagonia, has just been restored and can be visited. From Bagheria return on the motorway to **Palermo** (448km). ■

The Concordia temple in Agrigento

Car tour 7: CENTRAL SICILY

Agrigento • Caltanissetta • Enna • Aidone • Morgantina • Piazza Armerina • Villa del Casale • S. Michele di Ganzaria • Caltagirone • Ragusa

148km/92mi; 3-4 hours' driving

En route: Picnics (see pages 9-14) 21 and 22

Good roads take you quickly from Agrigento to Enna, Sicily's geographical centre. Enna is also connected to the Palermo/Catania motorway — a scenic road through central Sicily's extensive fields of grain. This tour goes to Ragusa via Piazza Armerina and Caltagirone, giving you the opportunity to link Car tour 6 with Car tour 8. The village of S. Michele di Ganzaria is a good overnight base.

Sicily is a fertile island. On this tour you will drive through central Sicily's sweeping fields of grain — landscapes that haven't changed much since antiquity, when Demeter was still worshiped in Enna. South of Enna, near Piazza Armerina, lies one of the most impressive Roman villas in Italy. Less well known, but also very beautiful, are the archaeological excavations in Morgantina, just a few kilometres to the east. In Caltagirone ceramics are not only shown in the museum: the whole town is decorated with *majolicas*, and excellent examples can be bought in many of the craft shops.

From **Agrigento★** (*i✝ℿ🏔✕🛒⊕M*) take the SS640 towards Caltanissetta. Without touching any other towns, the well-built road crosses fertile agricultural land. The vicinity of Canicattì is renowned for its Uva Italia table grapes. Do make a stop in the centre of the provincial capital, **Caltanissetta★** (58km *i✝🏔✕🛒⊕M*). A lively market is held in the maze of streets south of the Corso Vittorio Emanuele II every day except Sundays — a good place to shop for a picnic. Caltanissetta experienced an economic boom during the 19th century, when 80% of the world's sulphur supplies where mined in and exported from Sicily. The mines were closed a long time ago, but the *misteri* donated by the miners are still carried through the town in the Maundy Thursday procession.

Follow the SS122 and then the SS117^bis to Enna. Driving past abandoned mines, you cross the valley of the Imera Meridionale, also called the Fiume Salso because of the high salt content in the water. Seemingly endless fields of grain have covered the hills of central Sicily from time immemorial. And in the exact geographical centre of the island, Enna rises on top of a high plateau over these rolling hills. From **Enna Bassa** (78km) drive up the SP1 towards Enna. Take the first right turn, following signs for the Hotel Sicilia. Once in **Enna★** (82km *i✝🛆🏔✕🛒⊕🖼M*; Picnic 21), park in front of the Castello di Lombardia. You enjoy the best views from the highest tower in the castle or from the Rocca di Demetra (or Cerere). On a clear day, it seems as if you could touch Mount Etna. The castle or the Rocca are good spots for a picnic.

Return to **Enna Bassa** (86km) and follow the SS561 towards Piazza Armerina. **Pergusa** (91.5km 🏔✕), set at the eastern shore of the eponymous lake, is still a young town. To the ancient Greeks however, the lake was the scene where Hades, King of the Underworld, raped Persephone. Modern myths focus on the automobile, and so a racetrack has been built around the lake. From the **Bivio Ramata** (97km) follow the SS117bis again and the signs 'Villa del Casale'. (But if you are interested in industrial history, first visit the Parco Minerario Floristella-Grottacalda, just a few kilometres north of the junction: a hiking trail leads through this area of abandoned sulphur mines.)

At the Portella Grottacalda, the watershed between the Fiume Salso and the Simeto, the SS117bis turns south. On the way to the Villa del Casale, make a short detour to Morgantina. Turn off left (118km) towards Aidone. The small town, situated on a elevation of the eastern Monti Erei, developed around a 12th-century Norman castle. The archaeological museum at **Aidone★** (125km **i✝▲✕⛽⊕M**), where the findings from Morgantina are displayed, is worth seeing. It also boasts the world-famous Morganina Venus. The archaeological site of Morgantina lies just a few kilometres to the east of Aidone. A cobbled cul-de-sac road turns left off the SS288 and leads to the entrance of the **Scavi di Morgantina** (130km **π**✕wc; Picnic 22; photograph page 11).

Return to the SS117bis and continue towards Piazza Armerina (142km). When you reach the Hotel Villa Romana in **Piazza Armerina★** (144.5km **i✝▲** ✕⛽📷❀), turn right and follow signs to the **Villa Romana del Casale★** (149.5km **π**✕wc). This villa, dating from the times of the Roman Empire, is listed among the UNESCO World Heritage Sites.

From Piazza Armerina follow the SS117bis further south, as far as the **Bivio Gigliotti**, then turn left on the SS124 (170km) towards Caltagirone. The Hotel Pomara in **S. Michele di Ganzaria** (174km **▲**✕⛽) is renowned for its good cuisine. A landscape of rolling hills accompanies you on the way to **Caltagirone★** (188km **i✝▲**✕⛽ ⊕📷❀**M**) — Qal'at al Ghîrân ('mountain or castle of the vases') to the Moslems, who introduced the art of coloured ceramic glazes in the 9th century. The tradition still continues today, and you can make a good buy in one of the many ceramic shops.

Continue the tour towards Ragusa. South of Grammichele, an expressway takes you to the SS514 (207km), where you turn right to continue south. You enjoy a fine view to the Monti Iblei — a great limestone plateau stretching all the way to Syracuse. Take the **Ragusa Ovest exit** (240km) and follow the signs 'Ragusa Centro'. The Corso Italia leads you directly into the heart of **Ragusa★** (248km **i✝▲**✕⛽⊕📷❀**M**; Walk 40).

Mosaic floor in the bedroom of the Villa del Casale

Sell your books at sellbackyourBook.com!

Go to sellbackyourBook.com and get an instant price quote. We even pay the shipping - see what your old books are worth today!

00023442684

Car tour 8: SOUTHEASTERN SICILY AND THE MONTI IBLEI

Syracuse • Penisola della Maddalena • Noto • Noto Antica • Portopalo di Capo Passero • Ispica • Modica • Scicli • Donnafugata • Ragusa • Vizzini • Palazzolo Acreide • Pantalica • Syracuse

409km/254mi; 8-10 hours' driving

En route: Picnics (see pages 9-14) 23-27; Walks 36-41 (with accommodation tips)

On this route you will follow quiet, but mostly well-built secondary roads through the southeast of Sicily. If you stay longer in this part of the island, you will discover even more beautiful routes — a paradise for cyclists too. The cuisine of the region is well known, and some of the best agriturismi are located in this part of Sicily.

Politically the southeast equates to the provinces of Syracuse and Ragusa. The landscape is characterised by a wide limestone plateau, rising only a few hundred metres above sea level. Over the course of aeons, the rivers have dug deep, canyon-like ravines *(cave)* into this plateau. As early as the Stone Age, man had settled in these valleys, and impressive necropoli, hewn into the living rock, date from the Bronze Age. In the early Middle Ages, Byzantine monks looked for refuge in the *cave* and these 'cities of the dead' teemed with new life. The pale limestone, from which the towns are also built, reflects the sunlight very strongly, in a way unique to the southeastern part of the island. The year 1693 was a turning point in the southeast: a tremendous earthquake destroyed dozens of towns and villages, which were subsequently rebuilt in splendid baroque style. The baroque cities in the Val di Noto and later both Syracuse and the Pantalica necropolis (Walk 41) were declared UNESCO World Heritage Sites. The Siracusa tourist board has been expanding its network of hiking trails with the help of the CAI and the forestry commission.

Leave **Syracuse★** (*i☂⋔✝🛆⋄✕🖃⊕🖼M*) from the archaeological site: take the SS115 towards Noto and Ragusa. Past the Porto Grande you cross three watercourses in quick succession: the Anapo, the Ciane and the Canale Mammaiabica. Immediately after the bridges, a short cul-de-sac road to the right leads to the banks of the Ciane (Picnic 23; Walk 36).

No more than 1km further on, when you come to a lighthouse, turn left off the SS115. (But if you prefer not to take this short detour, continue along the SS115 straight to Noto.) Following the signs 'Villa Arlecchino' and 'Villa Lucia', you drive onto the **Penisola della Maddalena**. Over to the left, you have good views back over the Porto Grande to the Ortigia promontory and Syracuse. At a crossroads (8.5km), turn right inland, still following the signs 'Villa Arlecchino' and 'Villa Lucia'. Beautiful villas of the Siracusan nobility are set in these rural surroundings. Some, like the Villa Messina or Villa Lucia, take guests (🛆). At the little church (10km) drive half-left (this road is also used by the AST public transport buses). Turn left at a T-junction. After a couple of kilometres you encounter a crossroads (14km). Turn left and drive out to **Capo**

39

Murro di Porco, where the road ends in front of the lighthouse (15km). Behind the lighthouse the limestone plateau stretches to the sea; it's a lovely place for a picnic — when it's not windy!

Back at the crossroads, follow the signs 'Fontane Bianche'. When you're level with a grocer's store (19km), turn left towards Terrauzza. Fields with red earth, lemon and almond groves stretch behind the drystone walls. The road passes through the seaside resort of **Fontane Bianche** (▲△✕) with its fine sandy beaches. Shortly afterwards you meet the SS115 again (35km), where you turn left towards Noto.

Now the plateau of the Monti Iblei rises on your right. From **Avola** (▲✕🏨) you could take a detour to one of most spectacular *cave:* follow the SP4 as far as Avola Antica and, after another 3km, turn right to the belvedere (🕿; +26km return), from where you look down into the 280m deep Cava Grande del Cassibile. A trail leads from the belvedere down to the river, where the pools and basins in the bottom of the valley, dug out by the running water, are welcomely refreshing on hot days (2km/1.2mi; 1h15min).

The SS115 bypasses Avola to the west, then curves gently through the foothills of the Monti Iblei. Almonds are the main crop in this area. A bypass also leads round Noto, but go straight into the centre. Park at the eastern edge of **Noto★** (55km 🚻🛈▲✕🏨M), at the municipal park, then explore this interesting baroque town on foot. You must try the local almond specialities in the Caffè Sicilia, or the *granita* at Costanzo's Cafè Noir. The restaurants in Noto can be generally recommended.

From Noto the tour follows a very scenic route to Noto Antica, then makes a wide arc back to Noto. First take the SS287 towards Palazzolo Acreide. A few kilometres after **Corrado di Fuori** (🛈✕), turn left on the SP64 (66km). Driving past the old **S. Maria della Scala** convent, you reach the northern bastions of **Noto Antica★** on the plateau of Monte Alveria (70km 🏛🎪🕿; Picnic 24; Walk 37). A gravel road takes you through the Porta Montagna into the old town, which was destroyed by the 1693 earthquake and abandoned. There is a picnic area (🛋) outside the city walls.

Continue on the SP64, climbing towards Testa dell'Acqua. At the next crossroads, turn left (52.5km). The landscape here is typical of the Monti Iblei plateaus. Drystone walls, built with limestone, separate the pastures from the fields, carobs groves are frequent, and scented garrigue proliferates between the rocks. **Testa dell'Acqua** (56km) is little more than a road junction, with a small drinking water fountain in the square. From the western edge of the hamlet, continue left on the SP24, back towards Noto. From the plateau you look over the coastal plain to the sea. Monte Alveria appears to the east, and soon Noto comes into view once more. From this vantage point, you almost feel as if you were flying over the Monti Iblei. Past almond groves and the old cemetery, you reach the western edge of **Noto** (72km).

The next part of the route leads past the Vendicari nature reserve and to Ispica via Portopalo. Follow the southern bypass round Noto, then turn right on the SP19 (75km) towards Pachino. Heading south, you cross the valley of the Tellaro. Stop for a short visit to the Roman Villa del Tellaro with its splendid mosaics (**𝍌**)! Ahead you can already see the Isola di Capo Passero floating on a glistening sea. You pass the cul-de-sac road on the left leading to the main entrance of the Riserva Naturale Orientata di Vendicari (79km; Walk 38).

The SP19 continues through a dead-flat landscape of well-cultivated almond, olive, carob and lemon groves. The grapes which produce the local Nero di Pachino wine are also grown here. The vegetables ripen under foil and by early spring are ready for the markets in the north. Before reaching Pachino, turn off left towards Marzamemi. **Marzamemi★** (93km △✕) is a pleasant little fishing village with nice restaurants. The old *tonnara* (tuna factory) lies abandoned today. Nowadays, all the tuna is caught far out to sea, and the fish is processed on the ships themselves.

From Marzamemi continue south along the coast, past the abandoned salt-flats of Pachino. The Isola Capo Passero is clearly seen now. Turn off left at the northern edge of **Portopalo di Capo Passero** (100km ▲▲△✕🚐) and drive towards the 'centro'. Park in front of the Pizzeria Canarella or the Hotel Vittoria. A few steps lead down to the little port, where you could ask one of the fishermen for a ride over to the Isola di Capo Passero. The small island is completely overgrown by dwarf fan palms (*Chamaerops humilis*).

Back on the road, leave Portopalo by the church, turning right towards Pachino, which straddles the top of a low hill, surrounded by vineyards. The road through **Pachino** (107km ✛▲✕🚐) is a little confusing, so watch carefully for the signs to Ispica. Even from far away, the white buildings of Ispica shine out over the low hills. The deeply-etched valley to the east of the town is called the Cava d'Ispica. After crossing the railway you pick up the SS115 again (127km). Before you continue towards Modica, follow the sign-posting for 'Parco Forza', to make a short detour. Caves perforate the rock walls of the Cava d'Ispica: some of these Bronze Age tombs are used today as storage rooms and pens. Park the car just below the **Parco Forza★** (128.5km *i*𝍌✕🏕🚻wc; Picnic 25), where the town of Ispica stood before it was destroyed by the earthquake in 1693. From here you enjoy beautiful views over the surrounding landscape.

Return on the SS115, which you follow through the town of

Vendicari — the old tonnara *(Walk 38)*

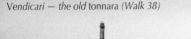

Ispica★ (*i☷※☎⊕*) towards Modica. Kilometres of dry stone walls criss-cross the landscape, drawing beautiful patterns. Watch for the sign 'Cava d'Ispica', and here turn right off the SS115 (142km). The road leads to the northern section of the **Cava d'Ispica★** (147km *i☷Ⅱ*WC), where you can visit ancient necropoli and Byzantine churches hewn from the rock. Following signposted secondary roads from here, you reach the centre of **Modica★** (158km *i☷▲※⊕🎞M*). Park on the Corso Umberto I and explore the town on foot — being sure to allow plenty of time. Don't miss the church of San Giorgio and be sure to try the traditional sweets and chocolates in the Antica Dolceria Bonaiuto.

Drive to the roundabout at the southern end of the Corso Umberto I (Piazza Rizzone). At the AGIP petrol station, turn right on Via Vittorio Veneto. Shortly afterwards, at a junction, turn left on Via Fiumara. This takes you under a high bridge and out of town. A narrow secondary road through the valley of the Fiumara di Modica takes you to **Scicli★** (170km*i☷◣※☎🎞*). Park in the centre. This small baroque town is not on the main tourist circuit but is well worth seeing. The Palazzo Beneventano, for instance, is certainly one of the most splendid baroque palaces of the region. Before the 1693 earthquake, Scicli was situated on the Colle di San Matteo, where the ruins of the Arabic/Norman castle can still be seen (Walk 39).

The route continues from Scicli via S. Croce Camarina to Donnafugata. Cross the valley of the Fiumara di Modica and head west, then turn left towards S. Croce Camarina shortly after the cemetery (173km). Trailing fine views back to Scicli, you reach a plateau. After crossing the wide Irminio Valley you regain the plateau and look down over a swathe of the coastal plain. Skirting to the north of S. Croce Camarina (194km), follow the road signs towards Vittoria and Comiso. At a roundabout (198km) turn right off the SP20, towards the 'Castello di Donnafugata'. You can already see the neo-Venetian façade of the castle rising above the pastures. The Castello di **Donnafugata★** (203.5km ◼※❀) and the beautifully-landscaped park can be visited (open daily, except Mondays, from 08.30-13.00; on some days open in the afternoons as well).

From the castle drive northwest a short way, looking down on the coastal plain south of Comiso and Vittoria. Vegetables are grown under foil, almost giving the impression of an inland sea. At the next crossroads (205km), turn right on the SP14 towards Ragusa. The drystone walls patterning the landscape are reminiscent of the walls of the labyrinth in Donnafugata's park. When you meet the SP52 by the restaurant Villa Castiglione (216km ※), turn right towards Ragusa. Passing through the western suburbs, follow signs for the 'centro'. The Corso Italia brings you into the heart of **Ragusa★** (224km *i☷▲※⊕M*). Follow the Corso Italia further downhill, past the S. Giovanni cathedral and the Montreal and

Left: the Chiesa di S. Giorgio in Modica; right: ancient theatre in Palazzolo Acreide (top) and balcony in Ragusa Ibla (bottom)

Rafael hotels. From a terrace above the church of S. Maria delle Scale (225km 📷), you enjoy the best views over Ragusa Ibla. From Ragusa the road zigzags down, with more fine views into the S. Leonardo Valley, to **Ragusa Ibla★** (226km 🚶‍♂️✕📷; Walk 40). Drive across the Piazza della Repubblica and past the Duomo di S. Giorgio to the Giardino Ibleo (227km 📷❀; Picnic 26; photograph page 11). The road turns right in front of the municipal park and leads out of town. You'll find a parking place here, if you haven't already. Return on foot and visit the lovely town at leisure.

From Ibla follow the SS194 through the Irminio Valley towards Vizzini. Shortly after **Giarratana**, you could take a detour left (+30km return) up to Chiaramonte Gulfi★ (🚶‍♂️🛏✕🅿📷❀), 'Sicily's balcony'. While the traditional Majore restaurant has been serving excellent pork dishes for more than a century, this detour is not only recommended at lunchtime; the town enjoys a splendid panorama!

The SS194 brings you to **Monterosso Almo★** (250km 🚶‍♂️✕🅿📷). Don't be deceived by the modern outskirts; drive up to the Piazza S. Giovanni. The core of the old town lies on top of the mountain and offers fine views. A scenic route leads on to **Vizzini★** (269km 🚶‍♂️🛏✕🅿📷), setting for the opera *Cavalleria Rusticana*. From here continue on the SS124 towards Syracuse. Monte Lauro, on your right, is a long-extinct volcano; on the left, Mount Etna rises over the plain of Catania. Drive through **Buccheri** (283km 🚶‍♂️⛰🛏✕🍴) and continue across the upper Anapo Valley to Palazzolo Acreide. A bypass skirts Palazzolo to the north, but take the first exit on the right and drive into the town to stop for a visit. **Palazzolo Acreide★** (300km 🚶‍♂️🏛⛰🛏✕🅿M) has some fine baroque buildings in its centre and the very interesting ethnographic museum, Paolino Ucello. The acropolis hill of ancient Akrai rises to the west of the old town, with a theatre dating from the 3rd century BC. Every year at the end of May students from all over Europe gather here to

Vizzini, setting for the opera Cavalleria Rusticana

perform classical plays. From the eastern edge of the town, continue along the SS124 as far as the turn-off left on the SP45 towards Cassaro and Ferla (313km).

Just after the bridge across the Anapo (327km) the road forks. The road to the right leads straight to Ferla; take the road to the left, which goes to Ferla via Cassaro. In the valley, Cassaro's old railway station marks the western entrance (*i*) to the Riserva Val Anapo — Pantalica. You can walk along the old railway track, following the course of the Anapo for 13km/8mi — as far as the old station at Sortino. Walk 41 follows part of this old railway track.

From **Ferla** (336km ♦♠✕⊟) take the signposted access road to Pantalica. The eastern end of the plateau, edged on the south by the Anapo Valley and to the north by the canyon of the Calcinara, was for more than 500 years the centre of the most important Bronze Age civilisation in Sicily. Shortly before the asphalted road ends, turn right on a gravel road which ends at a car park below the **Anaktoron★** (347km ∏⊡; Picnic 27; Walk 41). Several walks start from the Anaktoron, the ruins of a Bronze Age palace.

Return to **Ferla** (358km) and continue to **Sortino★** (378km *i*♦♠✕⊟). Pantalica can be reached from Sortino as well: a sign-posted cul-de-sac road descends towards 'Pantalica' into the Calcinara Valley (+12km return; Walk 41). Take the SP30 towards Mellili, then turn right on the SP25 (383km) towards Floridia. The road follows the crest of the Monti Climiti with breathtaking views, then descends into the Anapo Valley. The bright city of Syracuse is already visible on the horizon. Shortly before the bridge, turn left towards Priolo (394km) and, after a few kilometres, turn right on the SP46 towards Belvedere and Syracuse. At the eastern edge of **Belvedere** (402km), a short access road leads left to the **Castello Eurialo★** (*i*♦▮⊡; open daily from 09.00 until one hour before sunset). Visit this most important of the surviving Greek military works on foot. The position of the castle is well chosen strategically and of course offers a splendid panorama. In a short while you have reached **Syracuse** again (409km).

✺ Walking ───────────

There is no tradition of hiking as a leisure activity in Sicily. This is fully understandable, given that for generations farm workers had to either walk or ride a donkey long distances to reach their fields and olive groves. Travelling on foot was a sign of poverty, and today, when one says in Italian *facciamo una passegiata*, what is meant, of course, is a ride in the car! But time brings change. Many of the walks in this book follow old mule tracks, and gradually the word is starting to get around the tourist offices and the park administration that there are crazy foreigners around who *want* to walk and who want to see a Sicily beyond the temples and Taormina. As a result, new paths are now being created and the old mule tracks waymarked. We *stranieri* are setting an example.

The walks described in this book are as varied as Sicily's landscapes. You can stroll along a beach, with the scent of the maquis wafting on the breeze, or explore ancient ruins; you can hike through a shady forest or an alpine meadow, or scramble up a rock face; you can sail to islands floating on a shimmering turquoise sea, or climb an active volcano. There is something for everyone in Sicily. And walking in Sicily gives you the opportunity to experience one of the most ancient and varied cultural landscapes in the Mediterranean.

Waymarking, maps and grading

When the first edition of this book was published in 2001, there was very little **waymarking**, apart from a few marked trails in the Parco dello Zingaro, the Riserva di Vendicari, the Parco dell' Etna, and in some regions managed by the forestry service. Since then there has been some change; for example, the Forestry Commission has been quite active in the province of Syracuse. But the Parco dei Nebrodi and Parco delle Madonie could do more. The province of Palermo showed the greatest initiative of all, developing a network of waymarked trails and publishing corresponding hiking maps. But alas, their enthusiasm has not extended to *maintaining* these mapped, 'official' trails! Moreover, the last few years have been difficult economically and politically, which has affected general trail maintenance, so some signposts may well be missing when you are on your walk.

The Istituto Geografico Militare (IGM; www.igmi.org) publishes both 1:25,000 and 1:50,000 topographical **maps** of Sicily. With the exception of the Etna region, these maps are, however, sadly outdated. Litografia Artistica Cartografica (www.lac-cartografia.it) has published several hiking maps at 1:25,000 and 1:50,000 — including Etna, Madonie, Nebrodi and Zingaro.

The maps included in this book are sufficient for the walks I describe. But here are a couple of other useful maps I recommend, which can be obtained free while supplies last (see 'Useful addresses' on page 50).

- **Madonie — Itinerari nel Parco. Carta con descrizione sentieri** 1:50,000; Sicilia Outdoor & Parco delle Madonie.
- **Il Parco dei Nebrodi — Cartoguide Natura** 1:50,000; Touring Club Italiano & Parco dei Nebrodi.

All the walks in this book are **graded** according to the level of difficulty. This grading reflects not only the length and ascent/descent on the walk, but the nature of the terrain and the condition of the trails. There are six levels of difficulty: easy; easy-moderate; moderate; moderate-strenuous; strenuous and very strenuous. This is followed by a short description of the terrain and the condition of the trails. Even the most demanding routes should present no problems for experienced hikers. Most of the hikes rated easy-moderate are suitable for children.

Weather

An often-quoted phrase best describes when to visit Sicily: 'in spring, to marvel; in autumn, to savour'. Spring begins in February, with the blossoming of the almond trees; in March, one still has to reckon with occasional cold snaps; April and May are ideal months to walk and experience the intoxicating profusion of springtime flowers. In June, when temperatures rise into the 30s, the coastline and higher elevations continue to offer comfortable walking, especially if you set off early in the day or very late in the afternoon. From mid-September onwards, the temperatures are again moderate. October is well suited for both walks and swimming, and even the first days of November ('the little summer of S. Martino', similar to the Indian Summer), are usually very warm and sunny. Temperatures remain pleasant throughout November and December, even when it starts to rain. If you are well-dressed and equipped, you can go for beautiful walks (but remember to take the shorter day length into account). This can be a particularly good time of year to visit the archaeological sites.

Safety and equipment

Even the challenging hikes in this book will pose no problems for experienced hikers. Nevertheless, it is a good idea to start off slowly, letting yourself get accustomed to the climate and terrain. Unless you are doing one of the very easy walks, you should wear a pair of good ankle-high hiking boots with an adequate tread. It is not only safer, but also more enjoyable to walk without having to watch every step along the way. Protection from the sun and plenty to drink are both absolute musts on any hike. Even on sunny days, a walk at higher elevations calls for a pullover, windbreaker and cap to be stowed in the rucksack. If fog rolls in, it can get quite cool.

When hiking in autumn, it is important to remember that the days are shorter, so packing a torch is a good safety precaution.

At the start of each walk, I have briefly outlined the *minimum* equipment required. Here is an additional checklist: a first-aid kit, an elasticised bandage, an emergency blanket, a pocket knife, a telescopic walking stick and provisions. A **GPS** is always useful, if only for the track-back function! (But watch the sunflowerbooks. co.uk website and the author's website, www.walksicily.de, for free downloadable tracks from these walks.)

Ideally, one should never hike alone. If the weather shows signs of deteriorating, break off the walk and head back to base! Beware of thunderstorms in the mountains, especially on Etna!

Snakes, dogs and ticks

The only poisonous **snake** native to Sicily is the asp *(Vipera aspis)*, which can be recognised by its triangularly-shaped head and vertically-slit eyes. However, coming close enough to this snake to see its features is a rare occurrence! Most of the time, these snakes will flee at the sound of your footsteps. Vipers only bite when they are either stepped on or cornered. The large black snakes more frequently encountered are called yellow-green adders *(Coluber viridiflavius)*. (Despite their name, the ones you encounter in southern Italy are mostly black.) They defend themselves when threatened by inflicting severe bites, hence their name, but their bite is not poisonous.

Stray **dogs** may form packs in some areas of Sicily. They bark loudly but are not generally dangerous. Nonetheless, if you feel threatened, it is often enough to bend over, pick up a stone, and *pretend* you are going to throw it, to discourage them. If dogs worry you, you might wish to invest in an ultrasonic dog deterrent, a 'Dog Dazer'. For details, contact Sunflower Books, who sell them.

Ticks in the Mediterranean region may occasionally carry the bacteria *Rickettsai conorii*. This infection responds well to antibiotics and usually runs its course with no ill effects. The best protection against ticks is a pair of long trousers, especially when walking through high bushes or scrub.

Country code

Please keep the following countryside code in mind at all times:

- The land and its people should be treated with respect.
- Protect yourself and others from the danger of fire.
- Keep to public paths across farm land.
- Use gates and stiles to cross fences, hedges and stone walls.
- Keep dogs under close control.
- Take your litter home.
- Protect wildlife, plants and trees.
- Do not make unnecessary noise.

Where to stay

The Regione Siciliana (see 'Useful addresses', page 50) publishes a complete guide to accommodation in Sicily. Other guides are provided by the individual provinces (see 'Useful addresses'). In Sicily, the idea of *agriturismo*, or holidays on a farm, is growing more popular, and recent years have seen the growth of B&Bs. The following five websites may prove useful: www.agri turist.it, www.aighostels.com, www.bed-and-breakfast-sicily.it, www. camping.it and www.siculus.com.

Organisation of the walks

This book describes 41 main walks and a number of variations. More walk suggestions are in the Picnicking and Touring notes. A look at the fold-out map shows that some areas are more suitable for hiking than others. While the Aeolian and Egadi islands merit a visit of several days, they can also be easily reached on day trips, and I have described one walk each for the islands of Vulcano, Lipari, and Levanzo. Note that on these islands the traveller can — and sometimes must — make do without a car.

Every walk begins along the route of one of the eight car tours; in some cases, a short detour leads to the starting point. Only rarely can the trails be reached by public transport. For every car tour (except Car tour 7), I have included an average of five varied walks with different levels of difficulty. Taken together, they give a good overview of the region's diverse landscapes. Usually several walks can be reached from the places I recommend as overnight bases.

Begin by looking at the fold-out map and noting the walks that are nearest to you. Then turn to the appropriate route description where, at the top of the page, you will find planning information: distance, time, grade, equipment, how to get there and suggestions for shorter and longer walks. Modify the route as you like, to suit your own abilities and the weather conditions.

Throughout each walk description, **cumulative times** are given for reaching certain landmarks. These are only rough estimates, based on my own times, and making no allowance for rest stops. I recommend that you compare your own pace with mine on a number of short hikes before setting off on a longer trip. On long hikes, especially in unfamiliar terrain, you should avoid being caught in the dark. Most of the hikes are designed as half-day walks.

Below is a **key to the symbols and other features** used on the walking maps.

Symbol	Description	Symbol	Description	Symbol	Description	Elevation
═══	motorway	✝	church	⊟	picnic tables	0-200 m
═══	main road	⊶	spring, etc.	*i*	visitors' centre	200-500 m
───	secondary road	🖅	best views	✲	mill	500-1000 m
─ ─ ─	track.jeep/cart track	🚐	car parking	⌒	cave	1000-1500 m
-------	mule track.footpath	🚌	bus stop	P	picnic place (see pages 9-14)	1500-2000 m
2→	main walk	⊹	cemetery	△	starting point	2000-2500 m
2→	alternative route	■	building	400	height in metres	2500-3000 m
						over 3000 m

View from Monte Pellegrino towards Palermo and the Conca d'Oro (Walk 24)

GLOSSARY

Abbreviations

CAI (Club Alpino Italiano) — Italian Alpine Club
CAS (Club Alpino Siciliano) — Sicilian Alpine Club
SP (Strada Provinciale) — provincial road
SS (Strada Statale) — state road
STR (Servizio Turistico Regionale) — tourist board

Geographical names

l'abbazia — abbey
l'abbeveratoio — watering place
l'area attrezzata — picnic site
l'azienda agrituristica — country inn and restaurant
il baglio — fortified estate
il bivio — road junction
il bosco — wood
la cala — bay
il campo — field
la casa — house
la cascata — waterfall
la cava — quarry, gorge
la chiesa — church
la città — town, city
la colata lavica — lava stream
il colle — hill
la contrada — quarter (of a town)
la costa — coast
il cratere — crater
l'eremo — hermitage
la foce — estuary
il fiume — river
la fontana — fountain
il fontanile — watering place
la fonte — spring
la foresta — forest
la gola — gorge
la grotta — cave
l'incrocio — crossroads
l'isola — island
il lago — lake
il mare — sea
la masseria — farmstead
la montagna — mountain
il monte — mountain
la mulattiera — mule track
il mulino — mill
l'ovile — sheepfold
il paese — country, village
la pianura — plain
la pineta — pine forest
il pizzo — peak
il poggio — height, elevation
il ponte — bridge
la portella — mountain pass
la punta — spit of land
il rifugio — refuge, hut
la riserva — nature reserve
la roccia — rock
la rovina — ruin
il santuario — sanctuary
scavi (pl.) — archaeological digs
la sella — saddle
il sentiero — footpath
la spiaggia — beach
la strada bianca — gravel road
la strada provinciale — provincial road
la strada statale — state road
lo stretto — strait
la tonnara — place to catch and process tuna fish
la torre — tower
il torrente — torrent
la trazzera — mule track
la valle — valley

Directions

sempre dritto — straight ahead
a destra — to the right
a sinistra — to the left
attraverso — through, via
attraversare — to cross
salire/scendere — ascend/descend
qui — here
lì/là — there
da — from
davanti — in front
di fronte — opposite
dietro — behind
dopo — to
fino a — as far as
lontano — far
vicino — near, close by
sotto/sopra — under/above
su — on
verso — to, towards
il nord/il sud — north/south
l'ovest/l'est — west/east

USEFUL ADDRESSES

Tourist board, Italy
Italian Tourist Board
www.enit.it

Tourist Boards, Sicily
**Regione Siciliana,
  Assesorato Turismo**
90141 Palermo
Via E. Notarbartolo, 9
Tel. ++39/0917078201
www.regione.sicilia.it

Servizi Turistici Regionali
95024 Acireale (CT)
Via Oreste Scionti, 15
Tel. ++39/095891999
www.acirealeturismo.it

Aeolian Islands see Lipari

90015 Cefalù (PA)
Corso Ruggero, 77
Tel. ++39/0921421458

94100 Enna
Piazza N. Colajanni, 6
Tel. ++39/0935500875
www.ennaturismo.info

98055 Lipari (ME)
Corso V. Emanuele, 202
Tel. ++39/0909880095

98057 Milazzo (ME)
Piazza C. Duilio, 20
Tel. ++39/0909222865
www.aastmilazzo.it

95030 Nicolosi (CT)
Via Garibaldi, 63
Tel. ++39/095911595

90142 Palermo
Piazza Castelnuovo, 35
Tel. ++39/0916058111
www.turismopalermo.it

97100 Ragusa
Via Giordano Bruno 3
Tel. ++39/0932675837
www.provincia.ragusa.it

96100 Siracusa
Via Maestranza, 33
Tel. ++39/093464255

98039 Taormina (ME)
Corso V. Emanuele, 84
Tel. ++39/094223243
strtaormina@regione.sicilia.
it

91100 Trapani
Via Francesco d'Assisi, 27
Tel. ++39/092354551107/
24

Nature Reserves
www.parks.it/regione.
  sicilia/index.php
www.siciliaparchi.com

Parco delle Madonie
90027 Petralia Sottana (PA)
Corso Pietro Agliata, 16
www.parcodellemadonie.it

Parco dei Nebrodi
98076 Sant'Agata di
  Militello (ME)
Via Cosenz, 155
www.parcodeinebrodi.it

Parco dell'Etna
95030 Nicolosi (CT)
Via del Convento, 45
www.parcoetna.it

Parco Fluviale dell'Alcantara
Via dei Mulini
www.parcoalcantara.it

Riserva dello Zingaro
91014 Castellamare del
  Golfo (TP)
Via Segesta, 197
www.riservazingaro.it

Public transport
www.astsicilia.it
www.saistrasporti.it
www.orariautobus.it
www.circumetnea.it

Ferries and hydrofoils
Genova–Palermo
Grandi Navi Veloci
www.gnv.it

Napoli–Palermo
SNAV
www.snav.it/en
Tirrenia
www.tirrenia.it

Napoli–Catania
TTL-Lines
www.tttlines.it

Napoli–Aeolian Islands
SI.RE.MAR.
www.siremar.it

Salerno–Messina
Caronte & Tourist
www.carontetourist.it

Salerno–Palermo
Grimaldi Lines
www.grimaldi-ferries.com

Milazzo–Aeolian Islands
N.G.I.
www.ngi-spa.it
SI.RE.MAR.
www.siremar.it
Ustica Lines
www.usticalines.it

Trapani–Egadi Islands
SI.RE.MAR.
www.siremar.it
Ustica Lines
www.usticalines.it

Embassies/Consulates
UK: 00187 Roma
Via XX Settembre 80a
Tel. ++39/0642200001
http://ukinitaly.fco.gov.uk/en/

USA: 90143 Palermo
Via Vaccarini, 1
Tel. ++39/091305857
www.usembassy.gov

Walk 1: MONTI ROSSI

Distance: 3km/2mi; 1h20min
Grade: easy walk along a nature trail, with ascent and corresponding descent of 120m/395ft
Equipment: lightweight walking shoes
How to get there and return: 🚌 Heading north from Nicolosi (Car tour 1) fork left off the SP92 following signs 'Pineta di Monti Rossi' and 'Camping Etna' (△). Drive past the camp site and park where the road ends at a turning circle. There are some hotels in Nicolosi, but I recommend the *agriturismo* Azienda Trinità in nearby Mascalucia: a 17th-century manor with outbuildings in a beautiful garden with pool and views to Etna; tel.: 0957272156, www.aziendatrinita.it.
Note: The walk is a signposted nature trail and fitness path. There are picnic tables en route and, in the *pineta* near the Goethe monument, tables, barbecues and toilets.
Photo: view to Mount Etna from the Monti Rossi

On clear days the view from the rim of the Monti Rossi takes in the whole Etna massif, the Gulf of Catania, Syracuse in the south and the Monti Erei inland. These craters were formed during an eruption in 1669; there's a fresco depicting this event in the sacristy of Catania's cathedral. Along the SP92 a plaque at the foot of the Monti Rossi commemorates the German poet and writer Goethe. Accounts of his travels in Sicily during 1787 have been widely published. When he wanted to climb Mount Etna, a nobleman from Catania gave him the following advice: 'Most foreign visitors are too apt to consider the ascent a trifling affair. But we, who are near neighbours of the mountain, are content if we reach the summit once or twice in a lifetime ... If you follow my advice, you will ride early tomorrow morning to the foot of Monte Rosso and climb that hill: you will enjoy the most magnificent view and at the same time see the place where the lava of 1669 poured down on our unfortunate city.'

The walk begins behind the campground, where the road ends in a TURNING CIRCLE (825m/2705ft). Go through the green IRON BARRIER and follow the initially stone-paved road uphill. After just a few minutes take the path circling anti-clockwise to the right (WHITE-AND RED WAYMARKING POSTS). From the SADDLE (875m/2870ft; **30min**) you reach the PUNTO PANORAMICO SUD (870m/2855ft; **33min**) with a fine view to the neighbouring Monpilieri crater and the coast.

From here take the path to the left which winds up to a METAL CROSS and WATCHTOWER (933m/3060ft; **45min**), beyond which the trail descends again. Follow the rim of the crater down to the lowest point (880m/2885ft) and up again to the PUNTO PANORAMICO NORD (**55min**). A short climb to the left leads to another VIEWPOINT (946m/3100ft; **1h05min**). Enjoy the vast panorama to Mount Etna, before descending along the same route. Then head left, back to the TURNING CIRCLE (**1h20min**).

Walk 2: THE SUMMIT CRATERS AND THE VALLE DEL BOVE

See map pages 58-59   **Distance:** 10km/6.2mi; 3h40min

Grade: strenuous walk in full sun. The route is easily followed in clear weather but, if the weather becomes poor or foggy, turn back. You climb the summit craters at your own risk, so ask the local mountain guides (www.etnaguide.com) about current volcanic activity before setting off — or book a guided tour. Ascent of 340m/1115ft, up to a height of 3260m/10,700ft, mostly over volcanic cinder and sand; descent of 1350m/4430ft, mostly on sandy slopes. **NB:** At press date it was forbidden to climb above 2900m due to heavy eruptions in the summit crater area (see www.ct.ingv.it for latest news, but only in Italian).

Equipment: hiking boots, wind/waterproofs, spare layers and extra warm clothing, food and water

How to get there and return: 🚗 Park at the Rifugio Sapienza (Car tour 1). Then take the SITAS cable car to the Piccolo Rifugio and continue by SITAS jeep to the Torre del Filosofo (tel.: 095914141, www.funiviaetna.com; the one-way cable car and obligatory two-way jeep ride to the Torre del Filosofo costs about 40 euros). There is a bar and a WC in the mountain cable car station. Simple accommodation is available in the Rifugio Sapienza, tel.: 095915321, www.rifugiosapienza.com. The Hotel Corsaro has good cooking, too: Piazza Cantoniera, Etna Sud, tel.: 095914122, www.hotelcorsaro.it.

Alternative walks: 1) Circle the rims of the 2002-03 cinder cones below the Torre del Filosofo, then walk up to the *hornitos* formed in 2001 at the foot of the Cratere di Sud-Est and back (2.5km/1.5mi; 45min). 2) Follow the main walk to the Bocca Nuova an then down to the upper rim of the Valle del Bove (the 2h45min-point); cross back to the cable car station (8.5km/5.3 mi; 3h15min). Descend by cable car (don't miss the last trip down!).

The expulsion of gases and vapours is part of the normal volcanic activity of Mount Etna. When the magma column rises higher in the vent, additional magma particles are dragged along, which cool off in flight and solidify as bombs, scoria or ash. Eruptions happen frequently and last for hours, days, weeks or months. And it's not only the summit craters on Etna that erupt — chasms open out along the mountain's flanks and more cavities (called *bocche*) form along the chasms. Hundreds of these lateral craters cover Etna's slopes. Bocca Nuova, one of the four active summit craters, dates from an eruption in 1968. The Cratere di Sud-Est changed shape dramatically during frequent eruptions in 1998-2013.

Begin the walk at the **Torre del Filosofo** (2919m/9575ft), where all the jeeps stop. The old mountain hut was buried by the 2002 eruptions and has been replaced by the small Baita delle Guide. Follow the jeep track northwest. It leads up into a lifeless desert of slag and enters a surreal world, where clouds of vapour and smoke escape at irregular intervals from the summit craters to your right. The ground shakes after stronger explosions. On a clear day you'll enjoy a vast view over much of Sicily. After crossing a lava field from 2006, leave the track for a path on the right (2960m/9711ft; **15min**). Initially the path, marked by a WOODEN POST AND CAIRNS, follows the lava field to your right and than bends left. As the path narrows, it bends to the right and climbs towards the summit region, zigzagging steeply up during the final ascent. Suddenly and unexpectedly, the vast crater of the **Bocca Nuova** (3260m/10,692ft;

1h15min) opens up in front of you. For safety's sake, don't stay in the crater region too long, and don't stand too close to the rim.

Return the same way to the **Torre del Filosofo** (**2h**). From the 'Torre' signpost descend the SANDY SLOPE to the south, with the 2002-03 cinder cones to your right and the jeep track to your left. You'll cross the jeep track and pick up a path passing to the right of **Cisternazza** before reaching the upper rim of the **Valle del Bove** (2538m/8325ft; **2h45min**). A giant *caldera* opens in front of you here. The valley used to be a green oasis, pastureland: hence the name 'Valley of the Oxen'. But eruptions in 1991-92 blanketed the valley with a layer of new lava (the village of Zafferana Etnea barely escaped destruction in 2004-05 when more lava poured out).

The path continues by contouring, then descending the eastern slope of **La Montagnola** (2644m/8672ft). From up here you have a good view of the Crateri Silvestri, the main Etna road and the Rifugio Sapienza (**3h10min**). Descend the SANDY SLOPE: the path, unclear at first, continues in a hollow overgrown with cushion-like vegetation. The path swings to the right above the Monti Calcarazzi and young cones from 2001. When you meet the jeep track above Monte Silvestri Superiore, follow it to the right for a short way, back to the cable car station at the **Rifugio Sapienza** (1910m/6265ft; **3h40min**).

Left: the Valle del Bove; two of the summit craters: Bocca Nuova (top) and the Cratere di Sud-Est (above)

Walk 3: PIETRACANNONE AND THE VALLE DEL BOVE

See map pages 58-59   **Distance:** 6km/3.7mi; 2h25min

Grade: moderate-strenuous walk along forestry roads, old mule tracks and narrow woodland trails. Ascent and corresponding descent of 460m/1510ft. Route-finding after the 1h30min-point may be difficult in summer.

Equipment: hiking boots, windproofs, food and water

How to get there and return: 🚗 Park about 5km beyond Fornazzo, on a right-hand bend in the road (Car tour 1). The *agriturismo* La Cirasella, Via Trisciala 13, tel. 095968000, www.cirasellaetna.com lies isolated above the village of S. Alfio.

Shorter walk: Follow the cart track south from the Casa Pietracannone. When you reach the house which was nearly covered by lava in the 1979 eruptions (at the 2h05min-point), turn left and climb a path to the peak of Monte Fontana. You'll enjoy a vast panorama of the Valle del Bove and Mount Etna's summit craters. Return the same way (3km/1.9mi; 1h).

The scenic variety you encounter on this walk is extraordinary. The route takes you through mixed deciduous woods — a wonderful display of colour in autumn — up to the rim of the Valle del Bove. From the summit of Monte Scorsone you enjoy views into this giant *caldera* and towards Etna's summit craters. In the east the Costa dei Ciclopi is visible, while to the north the view stretches over Taormina and the Strait of Messina as far as Calabria.

Begin the walk at the bend where you parked. Descend to the right; the **Casa Pietracannone** (1150m/3772ft) stands on a slight rise to your left. After about 75m/yds take the right-hand track, cobbled initially. The peaks of Monte Scorsone and Monte Cerasa rise to the west — you will cross these mountains later on during the walk. The old forestry road ascends into a forest of chestnuts and downy oaks. As you reach a grove of aspens, you pass the 1971 lava flow (**15min**). Shortly afterwards, a short deviation to the right brings you to the large, lava-walled pit shown opposite. These pits, the *niviere*, were used in centuries past to collect Etna's snow, which was pressed into ice and used to make ice cream and cooling drinks, as well as for medicinal purposes.

Return to the main forestry road and continue 100m/yds to a FORK: take the cobbled track up to the right here, ignoring all side-tracks. A few weathered red and white flashes mark your way. As you ascend, the chestnuts give way to oaks and pine plantations. Where the track narrows to a path, follow green-painted poles and continue uphill in wide zigzags, until you reach the broad forestry road which leads up from the Strada Mareneve and crosses the lava flow dating from 1928 and 1971 (**35min**).

Follow this cobbled forestry road uphill through turkey oak woods, until you reach the **Case Paternò** (1334m/4375ft; **40min**), also known as Case Cubania. Stop for a break at this huge stone building, enjoying the fine view over Taormina.

Your route continues above the Case Paternò along the old cobbled mule track; quickly gaining height, you meet the broad forestry road again (**45min**). Follow it to the right. The deciduous wood here is rich in species — turkey oaks, beech, even the odd

54

Niviera at Pietracannone (top) and view from Pietracannone towards the summit craters on Mount Etna (below)

maple. The track climbs in deep hairpins, all the while overlooking the Costa dei Ciclopi. *Take care now* not to miss your TURN-OFF! About 30 minutes after leaving the Case Paternò, the forestry road (at this point with stone walls on both sides) makes a clear bend to the right (1465m/4806ft; **1h15min**). A few maple trees and a large BLOCK OF LAVA are to the left.

Leave the forestry road at this point and climb the path on your left, up towards the crest. A deep wooded valley lies on your left. The broad path swings to the left, passing a grove of aspens, then crosses a crest and the hollow of a valley. Down to your left you'll see Giarre with its harbour quay on the coast. Then you cross a fern- covered forest floor and come to the edge of the Valle del Bove, just on the ridge below **Monte Scorsone** (1603m/5258ft; **1h30min**). The giant *caldera* stretches out beneath your feet here, filled with the black lava from the 1991-92 eruptions. Rocca Capra and Rocca Musarra emerge like green islands from the solidified sea of lava. On a fine day you can see Mount Etna's summit craters straight across the Valle del Bove. This is a wonderful place to take a break, and I guarantee you'll never tire of the view.

Following the crest, now descend the narrow path. Take care not to lose sight of it — especially in summer, when the ferns grow high. After a few minutes it leaves the crest and winds down to the SADDLE between Monte Scorsone and Monte Cerasa (**1h45min**).

Continuing along the crest, a few steps take you up to **Monte Cerasa** (1531m/5022ft; **1h47min**), a wooded peak offering another fine view. It takes its name from the cherry *(cerasa)* trees that used to up grow here. Now the slopes are covered with chestnuts. The path descends to the east, again following the crest. If you loose sight of the path, just keep heading downhill to the east, until you meet a forestry track (**2h**). Turning right, follow this downhill until you reach a CROSSING (**2h05min**) in the midst of the 1979 lava flow. The house on the right above the crossing barely escaped being buried by the lava. The path going half-right here leads up to the peak of Monte Fontana (see Shorter walk).

To return, follow the wide track to the left down the lava-filled valley, which is flanked by ridges studded with chestnut trees. At the next two crossings keep straight ahead. The way is cobbled now and bordered by stone walls on both sides (**2h15min**). Passing chestnuts and apple groves, you return to your starting point at the **Casa Pietracannone** (**2h25min**).

Walk 4: MONTI SARTORIUS

See map pages 58-59
Distance: 3km/1.9mi; 1h10min
Grade: easy walk along a nature trail. Ascent/descent 100m/330ft
Equipment: lightweight walking shoes
How to get there and return: Take the short access road off the Strada Mareneve towards the Rifugio Citelli (Car tour 1). 🚗 park on the

right after a few hundred metres, at the forest barrier (there should be a indicating 'Monti Sartorius'). You can eat — and get valuable advice — at the nearby Rifugio Citelli (tel.: 095930000, mobile: 3489546409, www.rifugiocitelli.net, www.caipedara.it).

Photograph: Monti Sartorius

The seven volcanic craters of the Monti Sartorius lie all in a row like buttonholes *(bottoniera)*. They date from an eruption in 1865 and bear the name of the scientist who studied them, Sartorius von Waltershausen. Due to the altitude (the walk runs at 1600m/5250ft above sea level) the vegetation only took hold again timidly. But in sheltered areas you come upon little birch copses. The bright trunks of the birches (*Betula aetnensis*) contrast strikingly with the black lava. The most wonderful light effects are to be seen in autumn, of course, when the leaves are gold. A nature trail, marked with (now fading) yellow tags on wooden posts, takes you from viewpoint (*punto osservazione* PO) to viewpoint through this fascinating volcanic landscape.

The walk begins at the GREEN IRON BARRIER (1659m/5440ft): follow the wide sandy track into a light birch wood. In a few minutes you come to the first clearing. On the right there are the black ash cones of the Monti Sartorius. From between the trees you can see the mighty neighbouring crater of Monte Frumento delle Concazze, with the Pizzi Deneri (Walk 5) behind it. These views accompany you as the track climbs easily.

When you come to a larger clearing (PO2; **20min**), you'll spot some lava 'bombs' on the right. Then the track gently descends and crosses a little melt water valley. At the right of the track there's a small HOUSE built from lava, with a dilapidated sheepfold (1715m/5627ft; **30min**). Turn right off the wide sandy track here and follow the yellow-painted WOODEN POSTS (some may be missing) into the little birch wood. This takes you down into the melt-water valley, where you follow the route downhill for a few hundred metres/yards, before heading right, out of the valley (**40min**).

The path leads through a larger clearing and straight towards the black volcanic cones of the **Monti Sartorius**, crossing a lava flow. It climbs between two cones and up to a SADDLE (1700m/5577ft; **55min**; photograph above). Before descending again, walk a few metres to the left, to the rim of the crater, and enjoy the all-round view on offer: in the southwest are Etna's peaks, in the northwest Monte Nero (Walk 6), and in the north the Peloritani Mountains with the Rocca Novara (Walk 14).

The path descends south from the saddle, overlooking the Rifugio Citelli. When you meet the sandy track again, follow it to the left, back to the GREEN IRON BARRIER (**1h10min**).

Walk 5: PIZZI DENERI AND THE SUMMIT CRATERS

Distance: 21km/13mi; 8h45min

Grade: very strenuous. In good visibility orientation is easy; if the weather deteriorates, you should turn back. Bear in mind that the ascent to the summit is at your own risk, and before setting out you should let the people in the Rifugio Citelli know your plans. Ask about weather conditions and current volcanic activity! **NB:** At press date it was forbidden to climb above 2900m due to heavy eruptions in the summit crater area (see www.ct.ingv.it for latest news, but only in Italian). The ascent to the Pizzi Deneri is steep, and there is a long descent over sand from the Osservatorio Vulcanologico. Sometimes icy snow lies on the summits in early spring, making the descent dangerous without crampons. Ascent and corresponding descent of 1700m/5577ft

Equipment: walking boots, wind/sun protection, food and water

How to get there and return: 🚗 park at the Rifugio Citelli (Car tour 1), where you can eat if it's open. For accommodation suggestions, see Walks 3 and 6.

Shorter walk: Follow the main walk, but omit the climb to the summit craters. Climb from the Rifugio Citelli to the Serra delle Concazze and follow the ridge to the Pizzi Deneri, then descend the sand slopes from the Osservatorio Vulcanologico towards Monte Corvo and return to the Rifugio Citellli via the Rifugio Monte Baracca (12km/7.4mi; 5h).

Mount Etna is not only an active volcano, but a very *high* mountain, for which every mountain climber must have respect. Both facets of the mountain will become clear during this hike. As tough as the ascent to the Pizzi Deneri is, the visual rewards are great. Etna is not only the highest mountain in Sicily, but it rises in splendid isolation, so on a clear day the panoramic view is astounding. To approach Etna's summit craters is an awesome experience: they constantly gasp and smoke, and the air reeks of sulphur. Irregular explosions make the ground tremble and shudder. Before you ascend, take local advice!

The walk begins at the **Rifugio Citelli** (1741m/5710ft), where the Serra delle Concazze rises in front of you to the west. Follow the road a short way downhill and, at the end of the METAL BARRIER, turn left into the little birch wood. The narrow path, waymarked in places with WHITE DOTS, zigzags quickly uphill. You come to a CLEARING (**20min**), where the remains of a sheepfold can be seen by a tumbledown shelter. After 50m/yds, at a junction, take a right, soon leaving the birch wood behind. RED-PAINTED WOODEN POSTS mark a straight line, ascending parallel to the 1979 lava flow (the Rifugio Citelli is behind you). Milk-vetches (*Astragalus siculus*), endemic on Etna, form thorny cushions, green in spring and bright gold in summer. After crossing the lava flow to the right and then returning to the left of it, the path ascends further to the left and, when you're level with Monte Simone, reaches the **Serra delle Concazze** (2200m/7220ft; **1h20min**).

Here the gigantic black cauldron of the Valle del Bove opens up in front of you, with some craters rising from the valley floor. Ahead is the perfectly-formed cinder cone of Monte Simone. On a clear day the summit craters on Etna seem close enough to touch. Turning around, you look out over the Alcantara Valley to the Peloritani Mountains, Taormina, and the Strait of Messina.

After a well-deserved rest, make your way up the RIDGE (there is

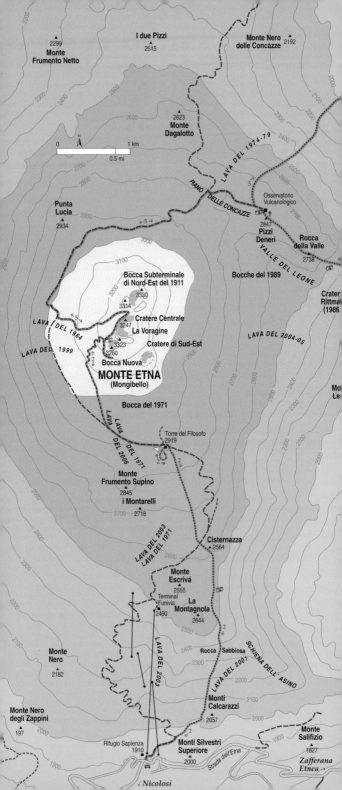

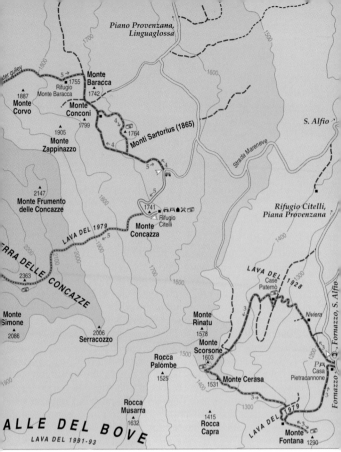

Piano Provenzana, Linguaglossa

1700

1600

1500

1800

5 ↗

1755
Rifugio
Monte Baracca

Monte Baracca
1742

1887
Monte Corvo

Monte Conconi
1799

Monti Sartorius (1865)

← 4

1764

← 4

S. Alfio

1905
Monte Zappinazzo

← 5

2147
Monte Frumento delle Concazze

LAVA DEL 1979

← 5

1741

Rifugio Citelli

Monte Concazze

Rifugio Citelli, Piana Provenzana

Strada Mareneve

1400

ERRA DELLE CONCAZZE

2363

2200

2100

2000

1900

1800

1700

1600

LAVA DEL 1928

Case Paternò

1300

Niviera

Monte Simone
2086

2006
Serracozzo

Monte Rinatu
1578

Monte Scorsone
1603

1500

Rocca Palombe
1525

Monte Cerasa
1531

Casa Pietracannone

P

Fornazzo, S. Alfio

Rocca Musarra
1632

1415
Rocca Capra

1300

LAVA DEL 1979

Monte Fontana 1290

Fornazzo

ALLE DEL BOVE

LAVA DEL 1991-93

a path). The steepest sections are made even more difficult by slag. As the ridge narrows, you enjoy views to both sides: to the left you overlook the Valle del Bove, to the right Monte Frumento delle Concazze and Monte Nero (Walk 6) on the far side of the Piano Provenzana. When it's really clear, you can even see the Aeolian Islands in the north. Beyond a first, dilapidated GROUP OF ANTENNAS (**2h50min**) the climb continues a bit less steeply, until you come to the highest of the **Pizzi Deneri** (2847m/ 9338ft; **3h10min**), marked with more ANTENNAS and a small METAL CROSS. On the far side of the Valle del Leone are the smoking summit craters.

Descend along the ridge to the white igloo-shaped building of the **Osservatorio Vulcanologico** (2818m/9243ft; **3h15min**). A desert-like plateau of black sand stretches out on the northwest side of the observatory — the **Piano delle Concazze**. Follow the track across the plateau, to a FORK (**3h30min**) where another track comes up from the Piano Provenzana. Follow it to the left uphill towards the summit craters. This ascent to the summit craters should only be made by very fit hikers and in excellent weather conditions.

Constantly gaining height, follow the track through a bizarre, fantastic lava landscape. Only lichen can grow on these inhos-

Above the Rifugio Citelli: milk-vetch cushions (Astragalus) and a view to the southeast crater

pitable heights. On clear days, half of Sicily is at your feet. Follow the main track to the point where it reaches its apex at approximately 3000m/9850ft (**5h**). Turn left here on the narrow path, which takes you up to the northern edge of the **Voragine Crater**. Sulphureous deposits edge the rim of the crater, above which there is almost always a cloud of smoke. **Bocca Nuova** (3260m/10,693ft; **5h20min**; Walk 2), further south, is another of the four active craters on the summit; it first developed in 1968. Take care here! Without going too close to the overhanging lip, walk a short way and then turn back after a while. There's always the possibility that explosions will belch some blocks of stone out into the air.

Retrace your steps back down to the **Piano delle Concazze** (**7h**). Just before the jeep track climbs back towards the observatory, turn left and follow the sunken terrain. With the solidified lava flow dating from 1974-79 to your left, descend the long RUN OF SAND. You look out over the half-moon of Monte Corvo to the Bay of Naxos. As you descend, keep making your way towards Monte Corvo. Look out for a CAIRN at approximately 1950m, where you cross the melt water gulley to your right. At the next CAIRN climb down the ridge between the two melt water gulleys. Then follow the gulley in the lava below the western flanks of Monte Corvo. There is water only after the thaw (and there is an alternative path to the right). At a height of about 1785m you pick up a sandy track to your right, which you follow a few minutes to the **Rifugio Monte Baracca** (1755m/5756ft; **8h**).

From the refuge, descend through pines until you come to a track, and follow it to the right. The trunks of these huge pines are sometimes serrated like fishbones (resin was once tapped here). The track soon crosses a MELT-WATER GULLEY. From here take the less evident, ascending track to the right, which soon runs through a dilapidated GATE. Now traversing the northern foothills of Monte Conconi, keep heading south. Shortly, you come to a little house built from blocks of lava, from where you follow the 'SENTIERO NATURA MONTI SARTORIUS' (Walk 4) in the reverse direction. Beyond the GREEN IRON BARRIER you meet the asphalt road (1659m/5440ft; **8h30min**), and turn right, back to the **Rifugio Citelli** (**8h45min**).

Walk 6: MONTE NERO AND GROTTA DEL GELO

See also photograph page 1   **Distance:** 19km/11.8mi; 5h10min

Grade: moderate-strenuous walk on forestry roads, narrow nature trails and across some pathless lava fields on the ascent to the Grotta del Gelo (in bad weather, you should not attempt the climb to the Grotta del Gelo). Ascent and corresponding descent of 700m/2297ft

Equipment: walking boots, wind/sun protection, food and water

How to get there and return: 🚗 park on the Piano Provenzana (Car tour 1). Accommodation suggestions: Rifugio Ragabo (tel.: 095647841, www.ragabo.it), at 1400m/4590ft, in the Pineta Ragabo on the Strada Mareneve towards Linguaglossa; modern hotel Il Nido dell'Etna (tel.: 095643404, www.ilnidodelletna.it) in Linguaglossa.

Shorter walks: Two shorter walks can be recommended: either walk to the Grotta dei Lamponi and back (8.5km/5.3mi; 3h) or make a short circuit round Monte Nero (3.5km/2.2mi; 1h15min).

This walk crosses one of Etna's most eye-catching lava fields. You'll most frequently come across broken-up lava blocks, the so-called 'AA'-type lava (the term originated in Hawaii). Its surface solidified during the eruptive flow, but then cracked again and broke up into rough strata. You will also see some *pahoehoe* lava — quite a rarity on Etna. This latter lava (photograph page 1) is more fluid. Like a gigantic mass of runny dough, *pahoehoe* lava forms interlaced coils and billowing rolls. Even after the outer coating cools and solidifies, the lava inside may still be warm and flowing, creating caves. The Grotta dei Lamponi is one of the longest of these caves. A small glacier came to rest in the Grotta del Gelo; when the snow melts, stalactites of ice form inside this cave.

The walk begins on the **Piano Provenzana** (1800m/5904ft), across from the STAR office (jeep excursions; mobile: 3474957091, www.funiviaetna.com). Follow the jeep track through the 2003 lava until you come to a WOODEN SIGN, 'Monte Nero — Rifugio Timparossa' (1905m/6248ft; **15min**), indicating a new path crossing the rough lava field to the right. CAIRNS mark the way. The bald cinder cone of **Monte Nero** rises up in front of you. The summit craters of Mount Etna are to your left, while the Nebrodi and Peloritani massifs rise to the right. Heading towards the cone, you

The bottoniera *at the 30min-point in the walk*

cross a small plain with cushions of milk vetch (*Astragalus siculus*) and another lava flow. Then the waymarked path turns 90° to the right (1935m/6348ft; **30min**). Passing a *bottoniera* (a grouping of about a dozen small craters along a line of 'buttonholes'), continue north until another path joins the path you are on. At this point turn 90° left (**35min**). At the next FORK (just past a tall lone pine and cairned; 1925m/6316ft; **45min**) you'll have to decide whether you are going to shorten the walk. If you are going to circle Monte Nero, turn left. If you are going to the Grotta dei Lamponi or the Grotta del Gelo (main walk), continue straight ahead.

The narrow path runs downhill through black scoria and then swings left. Crossing the hillside, you reach the edge of the woods (**1h**). Continue contouring through the wood, until you come to a CLEARING at the **Rifugio Timparossa** (1838m/6029ft; **1h05min**). The refuge is always kept open as an emergency shelter: there is firewood, water, and a medicine chest.

From the refuge follow the forestry track that runs down through the beech wood. On the descent you can already look down onto the Passo dei Dammusi. The track leaves the wood and emerges in open fields of lava. Soon the AA lava gives way to another kind of lava, *pahoehoe*. At the **Passo dei Dammusi** (1709m/5606ft; **1h35min**) you run into the PISTA ALTAMONTANA, which runs left towards Monte Spagnolo (Walk 7).

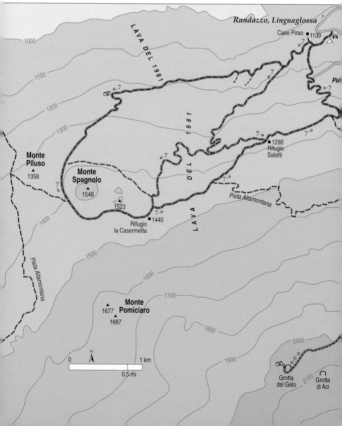

From this JUNCTION walk a few steps to the left, then turn left on a path which passes a first entrance to the Grotta dei Lamponi after just 20m/yds. Climbing higher (this path is marked with CAIRNS), you come to the second entrance to the **Grotta dei Lamponi**, at the point where the roof is caved-in (**1h40min**).

The ascent from here to the Grotta del Gelo should only be attempted in good weather; otherwise return to Monte Nero and pick up the main walk again at the 4h20min-point. The main walk continues southwest uphill. Solitary, wind-buckled pines have been able to take a foothold here and there in this bizarre lava landscape. Randazzo comes into sight, beyond wooded Monte S. Maria. You come to a plateau and finally cross a ridge covered with AA lava (**2h**). In the meantime the path is descending and passes a completely collapsed SHEEPFOLD and goes through a beech wood, before climbing another field of AA lava (**2h10min**). Then *pahoehoe* lava dominates the landscape again, always taking on bizarre shapes. On the final stretch the path runs over sand to the **Grotta del Gelo** (2043m/6701ft; **2h40min**).

If you go about 100m/yds north, past the cave, you will come to a beautiful panoramic view. Protected from the wind by chunks of lava, you can enjoy a view towards the Etna summits, Monte Spagnolo, the inland mountains and Monte Soro.

Now retrace your steps down past the **Grotta dei Lamponi**, to the PISTA ALTAMONTANA (**3h40min**). Turn right on this forestry track and climb to the **Rifugio Timparossa** (**4h10min**).

From the refuge cross the wood to the left and then take the narrow path across the dark field of lava, up to Monte Nero. Back at the FORK first encountered at the 45min-point (**4h30min**), turn right and round Monte Nero in an anti-clockwise direction. You may see the odd weathered YELLOW-PAINTED WOODEN POST on this path. Once on the flanks of Monte Nero, the path contours. You can see Etna's summit craters again; Monte Frumento delle Concazze is straight ahead, and to the left you overlook Taormina and the sea. The trail swings left and descends across sand to the point where the circuit is complete (**5h**).

Now follow the CAIRNS to the right and descend the jeep track back to the **Piano Provenzana** (**5h10min**).

Walk 7: MONTE SPAGNOLO AND THE CISTERNAZZA

See map pages 62-63

Distance: 13km/8mi; 3h30min

Grade: moderate walk, mostly on wide forestry tracks. Some forks are sign-posted. Ascent and corresponding descent of 300m/1000ft

Equipment: walking boots, food and water

How to get there and return: Take the Strada Mareneve from Linguaglossa towards 'Etna Sud' and after 3.5km turn right on a small road towards 'Randazzo' and 'Bronte'. After another 11km, at the bivio Pirao Superiore (915m/3002ft), turn left on the access road to Monte Spagnolo (by a basalt rock with the inscription 'Parco dell'Etna'). After about 4km turn right on a gravel road and 🚗 park in front of a wooden sign, 'Demanio Forestale Etna Giovanni Saletti' (if the barrier is up, just park in front of it). For accommodation try the friendly B&B Ai Tre Parchi (www.aitreparchibb.it) in Randazzo.

Shorter walk: Follow the main walk to the 15min-point, then turn left and climb a cart track for about 30min, until this rises to a crossing cart track. You can either turn left here — it's the shortest route to the Rifugio Saletti — or go right, across the 1981 lava field, to the Casermetta. From the Casermetta walk on to the Rifugio Saletti and return via the Piano Cavoli (8km/5mi; 2h45min).

On this walk you see for yourself the destructive power of Mount Etna. The young lava field that you cross several times dates from an especially violent eruption in 1981. After only a few days several fissures opened up in the caves lying between 1300m and 2250m, and lava spewed out, completely covering vegetable gardens, orchards, vineyards, farmhouses and even a stretch of the Circumetnea railway line (mentioned on page 8). One of the lava streams threatened the town of Randazzo for a while.

The walk begins at the gravelled CAR PARK (1139m/3736ft), in front of the FOREST BARRIER. Follow the forestry track west. After a few hundred metres/yards, a cart track comes down on the left from the Piano Cavoli (your return route later in the walk). Ignore it for the moment, and continue ahead on the wide track. The **Case Pirao** to your right are used as forestry houses. Again keep ahead at the next FORK (**15min**), where a cart track rises to the left, to the Rifugio Saletti (this is the shortest route to the refuge; see Shorter walk above). As the track briefly descends, ignore any turn-offs to the left. The forestry track rises again, emerges from the woods and crosses the 1981 LAVA FIELD (**30min**). Already there is a first feeble sign of plant life on this roughly-surfaced AA lava, but it will be hundreds of years before tall woodland grows here again. Scattered 'islands' of vegetation lie between the lava flows (see photograph opposite, left). There's a far-off view to the Nebrodi range from here, its crest covered with beech woods. Monte Soro is easily recognised, too, by the antennas at the top. The upper Alcantara Valley is visible beyond Randazzo.

The track passes an old drystone SHEPHERDS' SHELTER (**55min**). The area is still used for grazing, but not as much as in the past, since many of the old pastures have been afforested in recent years. The track rises more steeply in hairpins, while you look out over wooded Monte Spagnolo up to Etna's summit craters. At the next FORK keep straight ahead (**1h15min**). The forestry track makes a wide arc to the west round Monte Spagnolo, passing some new

On the northern side of Mount Etna: 'islands' of vegetation surrounded by AA lava (left), the Cisternazza (top left); Monte Spagnolo (top right)

plantations. A series of workmen's tracks join you from the left; ignore them all. In the meantime, the panorama now encompasses the Monti Erei in inland Sicily. In the woods a cart track comes in from the right (**1h40min**). Continue to the left, now on the south side of Monte Spagnolo. The track rises to its HIGHEST POINT, then starts to descend gently. Beyond a clearing, you come to the **Casermetta** (1440m/4723ft; **2h**). a ruined forestry house. Opposite it is a new refuge, which is always kept open as an emergency shelter. This is a good place to take a break.

Just a few metres beyond the Casermetta, you come to a FORK in the beech wood. Turn right on the cart track here, following the BLUE/WHITE FLASHES; it takes you back out of the wood. Since the forestry track was destroyed in the 1981 eruption, you cross the lava on a newly-laid path through a strange, endlessly-fascinating landscape — the ink-black lava field, the crevices which spewed out lava, and the branches of dead trees lying about on the ground like skeletons. Only a few steps further on you're back in a cosy wood and come to the hairpin bend of a crossing forestry track (**2h20min**). Turn left downhill here. Shortly afterwards you come to another CROSSING and the **Rifugio Saletti** (1290m/4231ft; **2h35min**). This unmanned refuge is always open — another good place for a break.

Keep straight ahead at this crossing, following signposts for 'CISTERNAZZA' and 'PIRAO'. The forestry track runs east through a leafy wood, mainly descending. The naked cinder flanks of Monte Colabasso fill the landscape ahead, and a track descending from Monte Santa Maria comes in from the right. After 200m/yds, where the forestry track describes a curve to the left (**2h55min**), you can take a short, but interesting detour. Follow the cart track to the right; in a few minutes this takes you to the **Cisternazza** (1337m/4385ft; **3h**). Although there is heavy rainfall, Mount Etna's stone is so porous that no springs arise, so the farmers and shepherds had to build cisterns. The circular Cisternazza, with a diameter of 9m/30ft, is the largest and most attractive of the cisterns on Etna.

Back on the forestry track (**3h05min**), descend with a fine view towards the mountains in the north of the island. Beyond the **Piano Cavoli** (1240m/4068ft; **3h20min**) take the track to the left, continuing the descent. The circuit is complete when you are above the **Case Pirao**. Turn right and, after a few hundred metres/yards, you're back at the CAR PARK (**3h30min**).

8: MONTE RUVOLO, MONTI TRE FRATI AND MONTE MINARDO

Distance: 12.4km/7.7mi; 2h55min

Grade: easy-moderate walk on well-built and signposted forestry roads. Ascent and corresponding descent of 250m/820ft

Equipment: stout walking shoes, sun protection, food and water

How to get there and return: Turn off the SS284 at the northern edge of Bronte, about 400m south of a supermarket. At the mini roundabout follow signs 'Hotel Parco dell'Etna' and 'Villa Etrusca', then take the next main road on the right, Viale Kennedy. This heads south out of the village, passing the restaurant Villa Etrusca' and the commercial zone. Further on the road becomes cobbled with lava and crosses the bizarre 1843 lava flow. Some 7.5km along, 🚗 park in front of the barrier at the Casermetta. The simple local Hotel Parco dell'Etna has good cooking (Contrada Borgonovo, tel.: 095691907, www.parco deletna.com). My particular suggestion is the hotel-restaurant La Fucina dell'Etna (Contrada Piano Palo/SS284, tel.: 095693730, www.hotelristoranteetna.it).

Alternative walks: The walk described can be shortened or lengthened as you like. You won't have any difficulty finding your way, since the tracks have been signposted by the forestry commission.

Bronte, a sprawling town with a centre dating from the Middle Ages, is best known for the cultivation of pistachios. It was the Arabs who introduced this exotic tree to Sicily. Bronte is the best place to find all the culinary specialities that can be concocted from pistachio nuts. Near Bronte is the former Abbey of Maniace (Car tour 3, photograph page 23), known as the Castello Nelson since the 18th century, when Admiral Nelson was made Duke of Bronte by the Bourbon King Ferdinand. This walk, just a few kilometres south of Bronte, takes you through a richly-varied crater landscape and the largest holm oak woods on Etna's flanks.

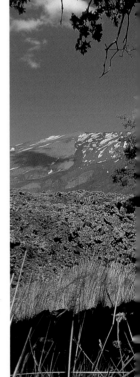

The walk begins at the **Casermetta**, a former forestry house (1156m/3792ft). Cross the LAVA WALL at the left of the gate and follow the wide sandy track towards Monte Ruvolo. The huge Etna broom bushes *(Genista aetnensis)* growing here gave their name to this plateau — **Piano delle Ginestra**. One of Etna's most beautiful crater landscapes spreads before you, where old volcanic cones, which have been wooded for many centuries, alternate with young black craters. At a FORK below Monte Ruvolo, continue to the left (sign-posted 'RIFUGIO M. RUVOLO'; **15min**).

Taking a picnic break with a view towards Monte Lepre

This track rises gently along the northern flank of **Monte Ruvolo**, with a view left to the Nebrodi range. At another FORK (**25min**), keep straight ahead. (A detour to the right here would take you in a few minutes to a stone house; it has been restored by the forestry workers and is a lovely place for a rest and picnic.)

The track continues undulating gently. The flanks of Monte Ruvolo are completely covered by Etna broom; a lava flow stretches out on your left. The track bends to the right, and bit by bit the summit craters of Etna come into view, as well as the black cinder cones of the Monti Nespoli, reddish Monte Nuovo and the wooded Monti Tre Frati. You come to a crossing track, which runs left towards Monte Lepre (1295m/4247ft; **45min**).

Turn right here and, after about 100m/yds, turn left on a track signposted to the 'MONTI TRE FRATI', shortly passing a small shrine on your left. This track runs across a wide lava field and into a wood of mixed oaks, before forking in a CLEARING (**55min**). Climb up to the left here. This track is cobbled in places and leads through denser woodland. The track forks again in another CLEARING (1313m/4306ft; **1h05min**) in front of a *pagghiaru*, a traditional forest shelter (see overleaf).

Continue to the right and cross the next, elongated CLEARING. A track joins from the right and, shortly afterwards, another track joins from the left (**1h10min**). Keeping to the same direction, go half-right here. The track narrows a bit, but always is wide enough for a cart. It runs through a holm oak wood with gentle ups and downs, until

Forestry workers' shelter (pagghiaru) in the Bosco di Centorbi

you come to a crossing forestry track at the **Case Zampini** (1344m/4408ft; **1h25min**).

Instead of descending the forestry track, take the old mule track at the right of it (there is a WOODEN FENCE at the outset). The trail runs through a GATE and zigzags downhill through a mixed oak wood, until it descends to a crossing forestry track (**1h35min**). Turn right on this track and continue downhill.

You pass another *pagghiaru*. The forestry track leads to a TRIANGULAR CLEARING (1202m/3943ft; **1h45min**), where a track on the right comes down from the **Monti Tre Frati**. Continue straight ahead here; then, after 50m/yds, at the next FORK, turn left.

As the forestry track descends between Monte Peloso and Monte Sellato, a track comes in from the left, from the Prato Fiorito (**1h55min**). Continue to the right here. On the left there are abandoned olive groves. A track joins from the right (1125m/3691ft; **2h**); there is another *pagghiaru* at this FORK. Keep descending to the left.

In a few minutes turn right on a track signposted to 'MONTE MINARDO' (**2h05min**). Gently ascending overall, this track enters a holm oak wood, where a myriad of cyclamen flower in autumn. Ignore a turn-off to the right (**2h10min**). By now the main track is gently descending and leaves the oak wood for a plateau full of broom. The route makes a wide arc round **Monte Minardo**. The track is now accompanied by a drystone wall.

Keep straight ahead, pass a first GATE (**2h30min**) and then another GATE (**2h40min**), ignoring the tracks branching off to the left. Now inside the fencing, you'll reach a crossing track (1149m/3769ft; **2h45min**). Follow the level track to the left, back to the starting point at the **Casermetta** (**2h55min**).

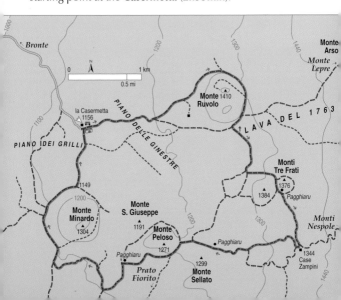

Walk 9: MONTE VENERE

Distance: 5km/3mi; 2h

Grade: moderate, with a steep ascent. The partly-signposted route follows little-used secondary roads, cobbled mule tracks, and goats' trails — all in full sun. Ascent/descent of 355m/1165ft

Equipment: hiking boots, sun protection, food and water

How to get there and return: 🚗 Park in Castelmola, or 🚌 from Taormina to Castelmola. Castelmola can also be reached on foot from Taormina (Car tour 2). There is, of course, plenty of accommodation in Taormina, including the Villa Schuler, Piazzetta Bastione 16, tel.: 094223481, www. villaschuler.com (the owner is an enthusiastic hiker!) and Pensione Villino Gallodoro, at the Bay of Mazzarò, Via Nazionale 147, tel.: 094223860, www.hotelgallodoro.it.

Shorter walks: Walk from Taormina to Castelmola; marvellous views accompany you on the ascent. In Taormina, climb the steps leading off the Via Circonvallazione up to the 'Madonna della Rocca'. From here, more steps lead up to the medieval castle (although this is often closed to visitors). Follow the road to Castelmola a short way, to a ceramics shop, then turn left. A concreted path and steps lead up to Castelmola (2km/1.9mi; 45 min). Return by bus (several daily, but *only* Mon-Sat). *Or take the bus to Castelmola and walk down!*

The classic excursion from Taormina is an outing to Castelmola. Sir Winston Churchill was only one of many who enjoyed the local almond wine and the wonderful view of Taormina and the Gulf of Naxos from the terrace of the Bar San Giorgio. The visitors' book at the bar reads like a *Who's Who* of the 20th century! If you follow the old mule tracks on Monte Venere, you will also move on literary ground. The amorous adventures of Frieda von Richthofen with a mule driver from Castelmola inspired her husband D. H. Lawrence to write *Lady Chatterley's Lover*. Perhaps best of all, it's likely that you will only have to share the marvellous views from the peak of Monte Venere (also called Monte Veneretta) with a few grazing goats. Shop for a picnic in Taormina or Castelmola.

The walk begins at the Piazza S. Antonio in **Castelmola** (530m/ 1738ft); from here you already have a good overview of your route:

you can see the road leading up the southeastern flank of Monte Venere. Descend to the large car park and take the road leading past the war memorial and CEMETERY. A rusty signpost shows the way to 'M. VENERE'. Climb the road to the left, which is partly concreted. The road rises in deep hairpin bends, past the houses of **Rocella**. Once above the houses, the road narrows and flattens out as it passes abandoned agricultural terraces. Beyond a small SADDLE, asphalt

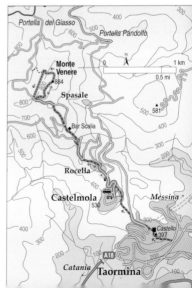

comes underfoot (**30min**). Follow the road for just a few metres/yards, then turn left on a narrow path which leads into a beautifully-built set of steps — an old mule track climbing the RIDGE. Shortly before the *mulattiera* is interrupted by the asphalt road, you can take a brief rest on a stone bench (**40min**).

Follow the asphalt road for a short while, until you can continue to the left on a path below a water tank (**45min**). Then cross the asphalt road. The partially-overgrown steps of the mule track lead past the pink ruins of the Bar Scalia. Cross the asphalt road and continue on the *mulattiera* along the RIDGE. On the slopes you can see abandoned terraces, serving only as pastures today. At a SADDLE, follow the narrow asphalt road to the left once again, until you reach the next SADDLE (890m/2920ft; **50min**).

Turn sharp right here, climbing a path over stone slabs and heading left into a large SADDLE. From this hollow a clear path takes you up to **Monte Venere** (885m/2903ft; **1h05min**), its peak marked by a stone pyramid. Few mountaintops in Sicily offer such a panorama — the Peloritani in the north, the Strait of Messina and Calabria in the east, Taormina and the Bay of Naxos at your feet and, in the south, the ever-present Etna. On a clear day the view stretches far as Syracuse.

Return the same way to **Castelmola** (**2h**). (Alternatively, you can descend the ridge to the north, following a narrow mule track towards the Portella del Giasso, then turn left to take an old mule trail on the western slope of Monte Venere. When you reach the 50min-point of the outgoing route, retrace your steps to Castelmola from there. See the map.)

Taormina and Castelmola (left); on Monte Venere (right); bottom: view from the Madonna della Rocca towards the Bay of Naxos and Mount Etna

Walk 10: FORZA D'AGRÒ

Distance: 7km/4.3mi; 2h20min

Grade: easy-moderate waymarked walk on asphalted and unsurfaced narrow country roads with little traffic. Ascent and corresponding descent of 220m/725ft

Equipment: hiking boots, sun protection, food, water, binoculars

How to get there and return: 10km north of Taormina, a road turns off the SS114 to Forza d'Agrò (Car tour 2); 4km of steep hairpin bends bring you to this small village. 🚗 park in the car park beyond the Chiesa Madre. Or 🚐 from Taormina (but scheduling is poor). Accommodation in Taormina (see Walk 9); in Forza d'Agrò try the B&B La Bouganville (www.bbcarnabuci.it).

Shorter walk: Take the steps from Forza d'Agrò up to the Norman castle, where there is a cemetery set in the midst of the medieval walls. The cemetery gate is, however, often closed (1km/0.6mi; 30min).

Forza d'Agrò is a great place to escape from touristic Taormina, and it's easily reached. Unfortunately, I'm not the only one to have found this refuge, so don't expect to be the *only* visitor! People in the little town are very hospitable, and many of them have worked abroad for years. Forza d'Agrò is built on the southeastern tip of the mountain ridge that this walk encircles. While a third of the route was asphalted during recent years, there is no traffic, and the views are still lovely.

The walk begins at the PARKING PLACE (365m/1197ft) behind the Chiesa Madre. Follow the narrow street which passes to the left of the church. With your back to the church, enter the heart of the old town along the Via Santissima Annunziata. You pass a bar, a grocer's shop and small streets leading up to the castle, and reach the northwestern boundary of the village (**10min**). Go left on the

Views near Forza d'Agrò, with tree spurge (top right)

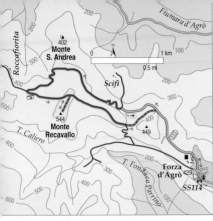

wide asphalt road here and, when you come to the FOOTBALL PITCH, turn right at the fork (**15min**). (For a short strech you could take the yellow-signposted trail parallel to the road.) You have a good view down to the right, over the Fiumara d'Agrò. With binoculars you will be able to get a better view of the beautiful masonry on the small Norman church of SS. Pietro e Paolo on the opposite side of the valley. The road widens out to a little *piazza*, where an old, oak-shaded mule track signposted 'ROCCA SCALA, RECAVALLO' descends from the left — this will be your return route later in the walk. For the moment, keep along the asphalt road, ignoring the cul-de-sac road off left to the cemetery (**30min**). The road descends gently to the next JUNCTION (**40min**). Turn left here and follow the hairpin bends uphill.

After a steep climb, the route — now a sandy cart track — rises gently in the shade of a little oak and chestnut wood. Lovely orchids and fritillaries bloom in the undergrowth in spring. Along the way you pass an old winepress. In the west, the small town of Rocca-fiorita is in view, at the foot of Monte Galfa. Beyond some pastures and an olive grove, you reach a crossing cart track (**1h20min**). Turn left here. After a final short ascent the track reaches its apex and a beautiful panorama unfolds before you: the mountain ridge ending in the village of Forza d'Agrò, a landscape of terraced slopes, Mount Etna in the south and, in the background, the glistening sea (510m/1673ft; **1h25min**). To crown this walk, follow the short path to your right, to the peak of **Monte Recavallo** (546m/1791ft; **1h35min**). On a clear day the panorama encompasses Mount Etna.

Back on the gravel road (or following sections of the old mule track beside it), descend to the point where the road starts to drop quickly in zigzags (at the foot of a steep rock face). Turn left here,

on a narrow path (420m/1378ft; **2h**). Steps hewn in the rock lead you up to a small SADDLE, from where you can see Forza d'Agrò again. Now take the old mule track running half-left down the slope and, when you regain the wide asphalt road (**2h 10min**), retrace your steps to the CAR PARK (**2h20min**).

Forza d'Agrò: the bright baroque facade of the Chiesa Madre towers above the small dwellings of the old town.

WALK 11: MONTE SCUDERI

Distance: 13km/8mi; 3h40min

Grade: strenuous, with some easy clambering involved. The middle part of the walk follows a narrow spine. Ascent and corresponding descent of 770m/2525ft

Equipment: hiking boots, sun protection, wind/waterproofs, food and water

How to get there and return: In Marina d'Itála (30km north of Taormina) turn off the SS114 to Itála. Follow the signs for 'Monte Scuderi', passing Itála and the turn-off to the Norman church of SS. Pietro e Palo. Park after 9.5km, in front of a little shrine in honour of Padre Pio; a metal sign indicates the 'Riserva naturale orientata Fiumedinisi e Monte Scuderi'. To return to the SS144 (+19km; Car tour 2), take the same road. The little Hotel Le Giare in Itála (tel.: 0909595006, www.legiare.org) is very welcoming. There are simple hotels with spas in Alì Terme, and of course Taormina offers a wide range of accommodation (see Walk 9).

The peak of Monte Scuderi is without doubt one of the most beautiful viewpoints in the Peloritani Mountains. Some might climb the mountain in the hope of finding gold. An old folk tale tells of a buried treasure on the peak. No one has found the treasure yet, and perhaps it was the golden glimmer of mica slate, frequent in this area, that gave birth to the legend. No gold mines, but snow pits — the *niviere* — are to be found on the heights. In the past, the snow was collected and pressed into ice in these pits. Then, in summer, it was carried on the backs of mules to Messina, to make *granita*, a refreshing sorbet concocted from lemons, almonds or mulberries.

Start the walk at the little SHRINE DEDICATED TO PADRE PIO (540m/1772ft): follow the broad gravel road uphill to your left, rising constantly in the shadow of chestnuts and downy oaks. On reaching a junction at a SADDLE, the **Portella Spiria** (676m/2217ft;

View from Monte Scuderi to the Straits of Messina

30min), continue on the gravel track to your right, now rising gently, parallel with the RIDGE. A tributary of the Torrente Alì cut the deep valley to the left. Further to the south you can see the distinctive plateau of Monte Venere (Walk 9), while the unmistakable peak of Monte Scuderi rises in front of you. From the next SADDLE you look into the Valle Cufolia to the north of the ridge and back to Itála. Shortly afterwards, the gravel track starts to climb in hairpins and your view alternates between the two valleys (**15min**). At the next JUNCTION (735m/2411ft; **50min**), turn right and continue climbing (the track to the left is your return route later in the walk). There is an information panel/map of the nature reserve here but, alas, it is of no great help). Shortly before the next saddle, turn left on a cart track (**1h**); a chain obstructs motorized traffic.

Just before you come to a small plateau with a derelict shepherd's shelter, turn right and follow the narrow, partly-overgrown path along the spine of the ridge. Some faded red/white CAI waymarks show the way to the peak, but you'll need some orienteering skills. In the south you can see the small mountain village Forza d'Agrò (Walk 10) above Capo S. Alessio. As you gain height, the path keeps to the left of the ridge and runs parallel with a fence. In the final part of the ascent, you cross towards the escarpment and a cutting in the rock, the **Porta del Monte** (1204m/3949ft; **2h**). The path leads through this natural gateway, past a little cave with a small statue of Sant'Agata and two *niviere* (snow pits), up to the extensive grazing areas on the summit plateau of **Monte Scuderi**. A little stone pyramid marks the PEAK (1253m/4110ft; **2h10min**). It is not so much the strain of the ascent taking your breath away, but the all-encompassing view from the top. In the south you look out to majestic Mount Etna, in the southwest you see the Rocca Novara, the highest peak in the Peloritani (Walk 14). You look down on Messina, the Strait, and Calabria. On a clear day you might even see the Aeolian Islands (Walks 12 and 13). A lovely place to picnic!

Retrace your steps to the second snow pit near the Porta del Monte and look out south for a breach in the low stone wall (1200m/3940ft; **2h20min**). From here take a narrow, slippery path zigzaging down the slope and continuing along the spine of the ridge (where it becomes somewhat broader). Cross down to the gravel track to your right (**2h45min**) and keep on going straight ahead. The broad gravel track circles Monte Votasana anti-clockwise and descends the valley of the Torrente Corvo in wide bends. At a crossing gravel track (**2h40min**) continue to the left. After a short while the track crosses the valley bottom (690m/2264ft; **2h55min**) and rises again, back to the junction first encountered at the 50min-point. From here retrace your steps to the Portella Spiria and the PADRE PIO SHRINE (**3h40min**).

Walk 12: THE GRAN CRATERE ON VULCANO

See photograph on page 2   **Distance:** 7km/4.3mi; 2h10min

Grade: moderate walk in full sun. Mostly sand, clay and scoria underfoot. Ascent/descent of 390m/1280ft. *Note: a small entrance fee is charged.*

Equipment: hiking boots, sun protection, wind/waterproofs, water

How to get there and return: 🚢 several times a day from Milazzo (Car tour 2). The crossing takes about 1h. From Vulcano there are many boats to neighbouring Lipari. Accommodation in Milazzo (best is the Petit Hotel; tel.: 0909286784, www.petithotel.it), on Vulcano and on Lipari.

Shorter walk: From the Porto di Levante walk past the warm sulphur pools to the sandy beach at the Porto di Ponente. Then it's a pretty stroll to the western side of the Vulcanello Peninsula. Narrow paths cut across the lava plateau. The views to the neighbouring islands of Lipari and Salina are particularly beautiful (4km/2.5mi; 1h20min).

The Aeolian Islands are of volcanic origin; Vulcano even gave its name to all fire mountains. The Gran Cratere is a textbook example of a volcano, with a perfect cone-shaped steaming crater. The last great eruption took place from 1888-90, the next is still expected. From the crater's edge you enjoy one of the most beautiful views on the archipelago (see photograph opposite).

The walk begins at the harbour, the **Porto di Levante**, where the ships and hydrofoils dock. Follow the asphalt road towards Piano, past the bar Ritrovo Remiggio, a little supermarket, and some holiday houses. The road contours along the foot of the Gran Cratere. Before reaching a large, isolated umbrella pine, turn left (**10min**). An easily-followed path leads directly up to the crater from here.

The path climbs the northwestern flank of the crater in deep hairpin bends. It rises from lower slopes overgrown with broom through black sand and finally traverses red clays. It's a lunar landscape, with large lava rocks that blasted out during the last eruption scattered everywhere. After a final bend in the path, you're at the RIM of the **Gran Cratere** (293m/961ft; **50min**). In front of you lies the perfectly-formed cauldron, puffing sulphureous steam. The most active fumaroles lie to your left. While it's very interesting to see the steam vents and sulphur-containing deposits from up close, don't stay in this poisonous atmosphere too long. And don't sit down on any sulphur: the acid would make holes in your clothes!

Follow the crater rim to the right, counterclockwise, up to the HIGHEST POINT (391m/1282ft; **1h10min**), where the whole archipelago is spread at your feet. On clear days you can even see Mount Etna on the Sicilian mainland.

With views over the green plateau of Piano, return the same way to the **Porto di Levante** (**2h10min**).

Walk 13: WESTERN LIPARI

See photograph page 21   **Distance:** 8.5km/5.3mi; 2h50min

Grade: moderate walk in full sun. Short sections of the walk are asphalted or concreted, but the route mainly follows unpaved roads and old mule tracks. Descent of 240m/790ft; ascent of 330m/1080ft

Equipment: hiking boots, sun protection, water

How to get there and return: 🚢 several times a day from Milazzo (Car tour 2). The crossing takes about 1h. It is possible to visit Lipari on a day-trip, but if you want to walk as well, plan well ahead (see the first paragraph below). There is a lot of good accommodation in Lipari. Pianoconte, the starting point for the walk, can be reached from Lipari town by public URSO 🚌 or by 🚗. Diana Brown offers very nice rooms in the old part of Lipari town, tel.: 0909812584, www.dianabrown.it.

Longer walk: The walk described ends in Quattropani, from where you can take the public URSO 🚌 back to Lipari. Alternatively, you can walk back to Pianoconte following a variation of the main walk. Follow the Strada Provinciale from Quattropani towards Pianoconte. Shortly after crossing a bridge over the Vallone Bianco, turn right on Via Caolino, following the signpost 'Cave di Caolino'. Heading west across the plateau of Castellaro, you reach the abandoned buildings of the kaolin mine (photograph page 21). The Timpone Pataso peak rises in front of you. Enjoying the view, descend the wide — and deeply eroded — road into the valley until you rejoin the coastal route. This takes you back to the Terme di S. Calogero. Climb the paved mule track back to Pianoconte (8km/5mi; 2h20min).

Lipari, the main island of the Aeolian archipelago, has a very varied landscape. This walk, along the west coast, could be easily combined with a bus tour round the island (but bear in mind that the public buses only make this circuit of the island during the summer season). However, you could try to hitch-hike from Quattropani to Acquacalda and take the bus back to Lipari from there. Bearing in mind that this excursion can take a whole day, *do* decide in advance whether you should stay overnight in Lipari.

The walk begins at the BUS STOP at the southern end of **Pianoconte** (280m/918ft). Turn into Via Palmeto; it passes the rose-coloured school on the left and heads west. The road cuts across the plateau, where scattered houses lie surrounded by fields of grain and gardens. Then the road descends between stone walls into a valley (**5min**). Over the green iron railings to your left, you can see the sea. The road rises again and passes through the group of small houses called **Varesana di Sotto** (**10min**). From the next valley floor, follow the concreted road ascending to the left, past the joiner's workshop. When the way forks by an isolated house (Casa Manfrè), continue straight ahead (**20min**). The narrow concrete road changes into a beautiful stone-paved mule track which zigzags down to the **Terme di S. Calogero** (141m/462ft; **45min**).

The asphalted cul-de-sac road from Pianoconte also ends in front of the spa. The big building is the restored thermal spa dating from the 19th century. But the ancient thermal baths on its eastern side are much more interesting. The Bronze Age dome is thought to be the oldest steam bath in the world, having been in use for over 3500 years.

The walk continues on the western side of the spa. From the asphalted road turn right on the concreted track, which leads past two palm trees and heads towards the sea. In front of you lie the western islands of the archipelago: Salina with its prominent double peak, Filicudi, and furthest to the west, Alicudi. Shortly after passing a solitary house, you can make a short detour. Take a sandy track to the left, going through a gap in the low wall. After a few metres you reach the edge of the cliff, from where there is a marvellous view to the island of Vulcano (**1h**). Back on the main track, the route curves into the **Vallone dei Lacci**. The track crosses the valley on a little BRIDGE and then undulates gently north, parallel with the coast. Along the way a dirt road joins from the right, from the abandoned kaolin mines at Timpone Pataso (**1h30min**). Shortly afterwards, a short cul-de-sac track branches off to the left to **Punta Palmeto** (40m/130ft; **1h35min**) — a nice place to take a short break, where you will see some of the dwarf fan palms *(Chamaerops humilis)* which have given the point its name.

Continue along the wide unsurfaced track, parallel with the coast (**1h40min**). After crossing the valley floor between **Timpone Palaso** and **Timpone Ospedale** (**1h50min**), the way narrows to a footpath. After a short ascent, you reach a further VALLEY FLOOR (**2h**). The path then rises with the slope and ascends more steeply in zigzags. Eventually the houses of the **Contrada Area Morta** come into view ahead, and the old mule track meets a concreted single-lane road (**2h25min**).

Follow the concreted road uphill to the right and, when the road bends to the left, go straight ahead on a cobbled track. On meeting the concreted road again, follow it to the left. The road bends to the right and reaches a CROSSROADS with a SHRINE dedicated to the Madonna: go straight ahead here. After a steep rise you meet the STRADA PROVINCIALE in **Quattropani** (369m/1210ft; **2h 50min**). The public bus back to Lipari stops here. There is a bar on the opposite side of the road and, a few metres to the left, the highly-recommended restaurant A Menza Quartara, another bar, and a little grocer's shop.

Walk 14: ROCCA NOVARA

See photograph page 20

Distance: 4km/2.5mi; 2h

Grade: moderate-strenuous, with a steep ascent to the peak. Gravel road, nature trails, partly over loose rocks. Ascent and corresponding descent of 366m/1200ft

Equipment: hiking boots, wind/waterproofs, food and water

How to get there and return: 🚗 Park at the Bivio Fondacheli, on the SS185, shortly after the km27,300 road-marker (Car tour 2).

Shorter walk: Avoid the final ascent to the peak; it's an easy walk to the foot of the Rocca, from where there are marvellous views (3km/1.9mi; 1h).

Rocca Novara, shown on page 20, is often called the 'Matterhorn of Sicily', and with good reason. This steep limestone rock towers proudly above all the other peaks in the Peloritani range. It's no wonder that a marvellous view awaits you at the top, but first you have to earn it. The last part of the ascent is steep and tough.

The walk begins at the **Bivio Fondacheli** (974m/3195ft) on the SS185. Walk back a few steps towards Novara di Sicilia, then turn right on a forestry track, into chestnuts and oaks. As the track rises with the RIDGE, another forestry track joins from the left. Leaving the woods behind, you come to a CROSSING (**10min**). With the fire-watchtower behind you, go straight uphill. To the right you overlook the wide valley of the Torrente Fantina, while the limestone crest culminating in Rocca Novara rises to the left.

The gravel track bends to the right and rises more gently now, towards a saddle (a path crosses a landslide interrupting the track). Beyond the saddle you can see the Tyrrhenian coast with Capo Tindari as a prominent landmark. From the crossing at the SADDLE (1135m/3734ft; **25min**), turn back west beside the barbed-wire fence. Change to the right-hand side of the FENCE and walk towards the steeply rising peak of the Rocca. The path forks in the next small SADDLE (**30min**). Follow the narrow path further up along the RIDGE.

The final (and steepest) ascent begins at a limestone gulley (1240m/4068ft; **45min**). A little caution is appropriate here, as the narrow path climbs in zigzags over loose rocks. The view from the TOP of **Rocca Novara** (1340m/4395ft; **1h**) is worth all the effort. If not the world, at least a good part of Sicily lies at your feet from this highest of the Peloritani peaks. Views you have already enjoyed from other mountains are seen from a new perspective: the silhouette of Etna rising in the south, hissing steam, the wooded mountains of the Nebrodi to the west, and the rugged Peloritani in the east, with their geological continuation, the Calabrian Aspromonte, on the far side of the Strait of Messina. The pretty village of Novara di Sicilia lies to the north and, on the coast, you can recognise the lagoons of Tyndaris and the Aeolian Islands floating on the sea.

Return to the **Bivio Fondacheli** the same way (**2h**).

Walk 15: MONTE SORO AND THE LAGO BIVIERE

Distance: 18km/11.2mi; 4h50min

Grade: moderate-strenuous. Short ascent on an asphalted road, forestry roads and trails. Ascent and corresponding descent of 500m/1640ft

Equipment: hiking boots, food, water

How to get there and return: At the Portella Femmina Morta (Car tour 3) turn off the SS289 towards Monte Soro and 🚗 park after 1.5km, at the Portella Calacudera. A former forestry house between San Fratello and Portella Femmina Morta has reopened as a hotel-restaurant; it's at the km28,660 road marker on the SS289 (Rifugio del Parco, località Casello Muto, tel.: 095697397, www. rifugiodelparco.com).

Shorter walk: Park on the SS289 at the Portella Femmina Morta. Then follow the cart track on the west side of the SS289 (a continuation of the mule track coming from the Portella Calacudera). It runs below stables and into a beech wood, gently undulating, parallel with the ridge on the right. At the point where the track is about to cross the ridge and go through a gate, turn left. Without going through the gate, in a few metres/yards you reach the peak of Solazzo (1530m/5018ft; 30min; Picnic 7). Return the same way (3km/2mi; 1h).

Alternative walk: The Portella Calacudera can also be reached on foot from the Portella Femmina Morta. A *trazzera* (old mule track) runs on the southern side of the road (+3km/1.9mi; 30min).

On this walk you rove through the extensive beech woods at the foot of Monte Soro, the highest peak of the Nebrodi (1847m/6058ft). In March, before the trees come into leaf, the forest floor is covered with the most marvellous spring flowers. Late autumn is also particularly beautiful, when the leaves turn yellow and red. The woods are interrupted by streams and clearings where livestock graze. You'll frequently encounter half-wild *Sanfratellani*, a local breed of horses introduced by the Normans during the Middle Ages

Lago Biviere, late in the afternoon

(photograph page 86). Lago Biviere is a paradise for birdwatchers.

The walk begins at the ROAD JUNCTION at the **Portella Calacudera** (1585m/5199ft). The asphalt road, flanked by two CONCRETE POSTS, continues uphill to the antennas on top of Monte Soro. To the left a wide gravel forestry track descends to the Lago Maulazzo — your return route later in the walk. First, follow the ascending asphalt road for approximately 2.5km/1.5mi. The road is used almost exclusively by staff maintaining the antennas on Monte Soro, so there's little traffic. Part-way up, a short-cut to the left avoids some bends in the road. At SPOT HEIGHT 1774m, shortly before the peak, the road bends sharply to the right (just a few minutes further ahead, the *acerone,* a giant sycamore *(Acer pseudoplatanus),* stands to the left of the road).

Turn left here on the wide gravel track (1790 m/5873ft; **50min**) which runs between wire fences and into the woods. After about 50m/ yds, you go through a WOODEN GATE. This forestry track at first descends in a northerly direction. Remains of the original cobbled paving stones can sometimes be seen underfoot. For the next hour you'll be walking beneath a canopy of beech trees. Stay on the main track. After crossing a stream and going through another WOODEN GATE (1640m/ 5381ft; **1h35min**), follow the track across an elongated clearing. Once back in the woods, the forestry track crosses a STONE-PAVED STREAMBED, ascends again and reaches a JUNCTION (**1h50min**). Here take the wider forestry track descending to the left. A little clearing grants you your first view towards Mount Etna and, a

short way further down, you reach a wide, open grazing area, the **Piano Basile** (1550m/5084ft; **2h**). A short break is called for here, to take in some superb views: Mount Etna in the east, and the Bosco di Mangalaviti (Walk 17), the Rocche del Crasto (Walk 18), the sea and the Aeolian Islands in front of you to the north.

Enjoying views towards the Rocche del Crasto, follow the cart track curving to the left across the Piano Basile. Back in the beech wood, descend steeply towards the lake, following the main track along the ridge. At a JUNCTION in one of the small clearings (**2h15min**), fork right. Shortly afterwards you'll get a first glimps of the lake. The route then bends left, runs past a stable building with a tiled roof, and meets a crossing track (**2h25min**). Take a sharp right on this track, down to **Lago Biviere** (1278m/4192ft).

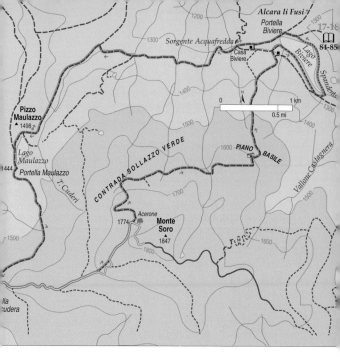

Follow the path along the southern shore; it is frequently used by the cattle. On a clear day, the peaks of Mount Etna are mirrored on the surface of the lake. A beech wood, mixed with holly (*Ilex acquifolium*), runs down to the shoreline. At the eastern end of the lake, turn left and follow a cart track through a GATE (**2h45min**). After a short ascent, turn left again and follow the path leading along the northern shore. Before reaching the western end of the lake, step over the STILE to the right, to join a wide gravel track at the **Portella Biviere** (1283m/4209ft; **3h**). A gravel track descending to Alcara li Fusi (Walk 17) branches off at this junction.

Turn left on the wide gravel track, heading west, passing below the Casa Biviere. If you're looking for drinking water, take the short detour to the right, down to the **Sorgente Aquafredda**. Back on the main track, continue uphill. Remains of the original cobbles are still to be seen. After crossing several streams, you come to a fork at a grazing area at the **Passo Taverna** (1360m/4462ft; **3h40min**). Continue to the left. The track rises slightly, with the **Torrente Cuderi** to your left. After crossing an elongated pasture, you reach a stone-built FOUNTAIN near the **Lago Maulazzo** (**4h**). The forestry track now ascends through light woods. Along the way a track branches off to the left, across the dam of the **Lago Maulazzo**. Go straight ahead here, following the fenced-in western shore of this beautifully-situated reservoir. Ignore the tracks diverting to the north. With your back to the lake (**4h10min**), climb the wide gravel track for another 2km/1.2mi, back to your starting point at the **Portella Calacudera** (**4h50min**).

Walk 16: CASCATA DEL CATAFURCO

Distance: 7km/4.3mi; 2h20min

Grade: easy signposted walk along an almost-level gravel track for the most part; at the end of the walk you follow a waymarked path and cross some rubble in a river bed. Ascent and corresponding descent of 100m/330ft

Equipment: lightweight hiking boots, sun protection, food and water, bathing things

How to get there and return: From Galati Mamertino (Car tour 3) follow the signs 'Pineta' and Campo' out of town towards S. Basilio. Follow the main road, with the tennis courts to your right, and 🚗 park in the right-hand bend, shortly before the road descends to the houses in the Contrada Galini. A metal cross stands on a rock here, and a gravel track turns off in the bend. A good place to stay is the Agriturismo Margherita (tel.: 0941435005, www.agriturismo margerita.com); to get there, turn north at the west end of Galati Mamertino towards the SS113 and Messina; it's then 2km down on the left.

You walk through a peaceful peasants' landscape in the valley of the San Basilio River. The stroll takes you to a waterfall, cascading from a height of 20m/60ft into a little pool. Bathing here is very refreshing on hot days.

Start the walk at the bend in the road (850m/2791ft) above the **Contrada Galini**. With your back to the METAL CROSS, follow the gravel track branching southeast off the asphalted road. Since you don't have to concentrate on route-finding, you can enjoy the landscape at leisure. The valley of the San Basilio stretches out in front of you while, to the right, across the valley, you might recognise the Portella Gazzana, Pizzo Mueli and Monte Soro (Walk 15). Without leaving the main route, you reach the little shepherds' settlement of **Molisa** (798m/2617ft; **25min**), at the foot of a steep escarpment. Up until a few years ago, the old stone huts still had their thatched roofs *(pagghiari)*; progress (and European money) brought the modern tile roofs. Beneath the rockface is a spring, the **Acqua della Rocca**.

Shrine with a statue of the Virgin Mary, just before the Cascata del Catafurco

The track forks in Molisa. The right-hand track leads down to the river. Continue by taking the left-hand fork, passing orchards and vegetable gardens, listening to the gentle murmur of the river below. (But if you come this way in spring, during the thaw, the San Basilio will be a wild and roaring torrent!) The track passes through the **Contrada Cannula** (820m/2690ft; **35min**), another settlement surrounded by orchards and gardens.

Past a STONE-BUILT TROUGH with cool water, you cross a tributary of the San Basilio (**40min**). Ignore the track branching off left through a gate here (it leads up to the Serra della Filicìa at 1228m/4029ft); keep on the main track. The gravel track rises and leads past a WATER TANK (a low concrete building with an iron door; **55min**).

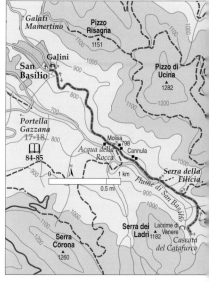

Leave the gravel track just *opposite* the water tank: take the signposted path down to the right, past a group of picnic tables. Where the valley narrows to a ravine, a few steps to the left lead to the **Lacrime di Venere**, a moss-covered little cave with a statue of the Virgin Mary. Further to the left, having crossed some rocks and rubble, you reach the **Cascata del Catafurco** (800m/2624ft; **1h10min**). On a hot day, a paddle beneath this pretty waterfall is irresistible.

Then, enjoying a view to the Rocche del Crasto (Walk 18), return the same way to your starting point at the METAL CROSS (**2h20min**).

Molisa: up until just a few years ago, the old stone huts were attractively thatched.

Walk 17: THE BOSCO DI MANGALAVITI AND THE LAGO BIVIERE

Distance: 17km/10.5mi; 4h40min

Grade: moderate-strenuous walk on gravelled forestry tracks and farm tracks. Unmarked, partly overgrown, steep ascent out of the Vallone Pistone back to the Case Mangalaviti. Ascent and corresponding descent of 400m/1310ft

Equipment: hiking boots, sun protection, food, water bottle (there are places to take on water en route)

How to get there and return: From the Portella Gazzana (Car tour 3) drive south along the narrow asphalted road. Without turning off, after 4km ⛟ park in front of the ruins of the Case Mangalaviti. The *agriturismo* in Galati Mamertino is recommended (Walk 16), as is Nebrodi B&B in Longi (see Walk 18).

Shorter walks: The surroundings of the Case Mangalaviti offer many possibilities for easy walks, suitable for children. One suggestion is shown on the map.

Extensive oak and beech woods, occasionally interrupted by clearings, cover the northern slopes of the Nebrodi. Along the way you will probably meet herds of cattle, pigs and horses. On hot days the animals gather along the southern shore of the Lago Biviere in the shade of the trees. The lake is also a magnet for birdwatchers.

Start the walk at the **Case Mangalaviti** (1256m/ 4120ft). There is a TROUGH here, where you can fill your bottles. Ascending the gravel track and leaving the light oak woods behind, you enter the beech woods and reach the **Portella Scafi** (1468m/4815ft; **1h**), the HIGHEST POINT of the walk.

The track runs through a GATE and begins to descend. After 200m/yds you meet a crossing forestry track. Follow it to the right, passing through another GATE. Monte Soro rises in the southwest. At first the gravel track runs across flat scrubby pastures, then it descends gently into a light beech wood. Along the way views open out over the valley of the Torrente Rosmarino and to the Rocche del Crasto. After a short ascent, you see the Lago Biviere spread out in front of you. Large turkey oaks *(Quercus cerris)* grow along the side of the track. Shortly before reaching the JUNCTION at the **Portella Biviere** (1283m/ 4208ft; **2h**), look out for a resting place on the ridge in the shade of the oaks. The view is wonderful: Mount Etna and Monte Soro are behind you, and there is a fine view north across the wide sweep of the Rosmarino Valley to the imposing Rocche del Crasto (Walk 18) and the blue sea beyond.

From the Portella Biviere (where you could step over the STILE to the left and reach the shore of the lake to join Walk 15), turn right on the gravel track descending in a northerly direction. Trees on the pastures offer shade to

84

the grazing animals. You'll pass a number of TROUGHS along here. The track runs across the **Piano Cerasa** (1117m/3664ft; **2h30min**), where there is a shepherds' hut on the right. Every morning from spring to autumn, fresh ricotta cheese is made here.

Shortly after the Piano Cerasa a two-wheeled track joins from the right. Keep to the main track, which descends in a curve to the left (ignore another track which soon branches off to the right). The track acquires a rougher gravel surface and descends more steeply. Ignore a number of minor tracks branching off, until you come to a JUNCTION at the **Piano Perotta** (867m/2844ft; **3h20min**).

The wider track here descends left towards Alcara li Fusi. Turn right on the gently-rising gravel track. Go straight ahead past a cluster of houses (**3h40min**). Another cart track joins from the right. Cross the FLOOR OF A VALLEY, turn right uphill at the following JUNCTION and, soon afterwards, at the next JUNCTION, go straight

ahead. The track ends at the **Casa Macchiazza** (991m/3250ft; **4h**).

Walk round the house and descend the narrow path into the **Vallone Pistone**. While the river is impassable in winter, from late spring on you can cross without getting your feet wet (**4h10min**).

The ascent back to the Case Mangalaviti requires a little orientation and patience, especially if you don't find the right path at the outset. As the map shows, the Case Manga-laviti lie some 250m/850ft higher than the Casa Machiazza, on the opposite side of the valley. Shepherds' paths branch off in all directions up the slope. It is planned to way-mark the most prominent path in the future for hikers. After a strenuous ascent, you're back at the **Case Mangalaviti** (**4h40min**).

Top: near Alcara li Fusi (Walk 18); left: half-wild Sanfrattelani horses; below: shepherd's hut (Rifugio del Sole) near the Rocche del Crasto (Walk 18).

Walk 18: ROCCHE DEL CRASTO

Map pages 84-85; photographs opposite **Distance:** 8km/5mi; 3h10min

Grade: moderate-strenuous walk on gravel tracks and some stony paths. Ascent and corresponding descent of 330m/1080ft

Equipment: hiking boots, wind and sun protection, binoculars, food, water bottle (there is a watering place half-way along)

How to get there and return: 🚗 park in front of the Ristorante Portella Gazzana at the Portella Gazzana (Car tour 3). Accommodation in Longi: Nebrodi B&B (tel.: 0941485068, www.nebrodibandb.it); they also organise guided walks.

Shorter walk: You can reach the Rocche del Crasto by following the gravel track along the ridge. When you come to the Bosco Soprano (30min) continue straight ahead uphill. The track ascends in hairpins and bends left after a trough, crossing a farmed plateau. It's quite easy to cross the plateau over to the Rocche del Crasto. Return the same way (7.5km/4.7mi; 2h45min).

According to legend, one of Aeneas' companions founded a town on the Rocche del Crasto after the flight from Troy. The site was well chosen, as this mountain fortress would have been easy to defend. Today eagles nest in the inaccessible places, with binoculars you might be lucky enough to see them.

The walk begins at the SADDLE, the **Portella Gazzana** (979m/ 3211ft). With your back to the restaurant of the same name, follow the gravel track northwest uphill. The track leads along the RIDGE which runs up to the Rocche del Crasto. After a few hundred metres/yards continue straight ahead, ignoring the track off to the left. You pass below a well-kept rubbish tip. Shortly after, at the next JUNCTION (**10min**), continue along the ridge.

At the **Bosco Soprano** (1090m/3576ft; **30min**), a forestry track goes right into the woods, while the gravel track runs straight ahead towards the Rocche del Crasto (this is your return route, and you keep straight ahead here for the Shorter walk). The main walk turns *left* at this JUNCTION, descending a partly-overgrown track which zigzags down the slope and runs through a GATE. Inside the gated area, another track joins from the left, coming up from the valley. Your track, which is making for the Rocche del Crasto, passes in front of a TROUGH (1000m/3281ft; **50min**), narrows to a path and crosses a little VALLEY. At the next JUNCTION, walk right uphill, between fences. Continue at the foot of the escarpment until you come to a little PLATEAU (**1h10min**). Through the ravine you can look down on Alcara li Fusi. To the left, the rock walls of the Rocca Calanna rise up vertically from the valley floor. Eagles build their nests here in inaccessible places. To your right, just as steep, is the escarpment of the Rocche del Crasto.

A rocky path, protected by iron railings, leads right uphill from the little plateau. After a few minutes you reach a small meadow. The next section requires a little orientation (the CAIRNS will help). Take the path climbing between the bright limestone rocks and some high tufts of grass. This leads up to the southwestern end of the Rocche del Crasto (**1h45min**). From here take the path to the left, running along the northwestern EDGE OF THE PLATEAU. To your left, behind the fence and across the valley, you see an isolated shepherds' hut and Pizzo Aglio (1251m). Once at the northeastern end of the plateau, you come to another (usually dry) TROUGH (**2h**). From here a clear path leads uphill to the right, to the SUMMIT of **Rocche del Crasto** (1315m/4314ft; **2h10min**).

From the summit retrace your steps and go straight ahead past the trough. Crossing a small patch of cultivated land, you meet a crossing track (**2h20min**). The isolated shepherds' hut seen earlier (**Rifugio del Sole**) lies a few hundred metres to your left; it's open, and you can use the kitchen to prepare a coffee, etc, but please leave a small tip! From here you can look down into the valley of the Torrente Rosmarino and towards Alcara li Fusi one last time.

With your back to the shepherds' hut and Pizzo Aglio, turn east and follow the track across the cultivated plain. After a few minutes, the track turns right and runs above another TROUGH (**2h25min**). Galati Mamertino lies across the valley to your left. After a short ascent to a saddle, the gravel track starts to descend, and a wide panorama unfolds ahead: Pizzo Mueli, the Bosco di Mangalaviti (Walk 17), Monto Soro and Mount Etna. The track leads past the **Bosco Soprano** (**2h45min**), from where you descend your outgoing route back to the **Portella Gazzana** (**3h10min**).

The castle rock of Cefalù (Walk 19).

Walk 19: THE CASTLE ROCK OF CEFALÙ

See also photos opposite, page 27 and cover   Distance: 4.5km/2.8mi; 2h

Grade: easy-moderate walk, on steps and narrow nature trails. Ascent and corresponding descent of 250m/820ft. *Note: The ruins are open from 09.00 until an hour before sunset; an entrance fee was under consideration at press date.*

Equipment: hiking boots, sun protection, food and water

How to get there and return: 🚃 park on the Lungomare Giardina west of Cefalù's old town, or near the *faro* (lighthouse) to the east of the old town (Car tour 4). I recommend a B&B in the old town: La Dolce Vita, Via Bordonaro, tel.: 0921923151, www.dolcevitabb.it. There are several hotels in the Calura district, by the sea, including the sports hotel Kalura, Via Cavallaro 13, tel.: 0921421354, www.hotel-kalura.com.

Cefalù has an unmistakable silhouette. The mighty Norman cathedral towers above the tiled roofs of the old town, with the impressive Rocca di Cefalù behind it. Follow the pretty alleys and explore the little port and the medieval wash house. The cathedral, with its marvellous mosaic decoration, was built at the behest of King Roger II in the 12th century. The Museo Mandralisca (open daily from 09.00-12.30 and from 15.30-18.00) is also worth a visit: Baron Enrico Piraino di Mandralisca, a 19th-century scholar with wide-ranging interests, brought together an impressive collection. Apart from valuable ancient coins, 20,000 shells, and ceramics from Lipari, the museum holds the portrait 'of an unknown man', a 15th-century masterpiece by Antonello da Messina. It's ideal to combine a visit to Cefalù with a walk up to the Rocca di Cefalù, the northernmost spur of the Madonie Mountains.

The walk begins at the **Piazza Duomo** (25m/85ft). Stroll south along the Corso Ruggiero, past the medieval Osterio Magno and the TOURIST OFFICE. Then turn left into Viccolo dei Saraceni, where a yellow metal sign shows the way to the 'TEMPIO DI DIANA'. Climb the iron staircase and follow the stepped ramp out of the town. After a few steps, take another set of steps up to the left, zigzagging steeply up the mountain. The steps ascend between the high rock walls of the valley, passing through several defence walls. When the way forks by a large CISTERN (**20min**), go left uphill, past the remains of more walls, cisterns, and ovens *(forni)*. From a small plain, continue straight ahead (north), until you see the ruins of the megalithic walls of the **Diana Temple** (9th century BC) on your right. Keeping this interesting building to your right, continue a short way north along the path, to a lovely VIEWPOINT (140m/459ft; **30min**). Over the castellated walls you can look down on the old town with its imposing cathedral, and the blue sea stretching out in the background.

From here follow the narrow path along the defence wall in a clockwise direction round the mountain, with more marvellous views towards the north coast and the Madonie Mountains. (Should this route be closed off, there is a short-cut up to the castle ruins from the Diana Temple.) On the western slope you meet a crossing path (**1h**). Before descending to the left, you might want to climb the peak. If so, climb up to the **castle ruins** (270m/886ft; **1h15min**).

View from the Rocca di Cefalù (Picnic 10)

The defiant-looking castle dates from Norman times and was enlarged in the 12th century. On a clear day, the view stretches as far as the Aeolian Islands.

Descend to the JUNCTION by the large cistern, and follow the steps down through the bastions. Reaching the edge of the old town again, turn right, without descending the iron steps to the Corso. This narrow alley, at the foot of the steep rock wall, takes you straight back to the **Piazza Duomo** (**2h**). Take another look at the apses in the cathedral, and you'll see some amusing small sculptures. More of the stonemasons' art is to be seen in the cloister.

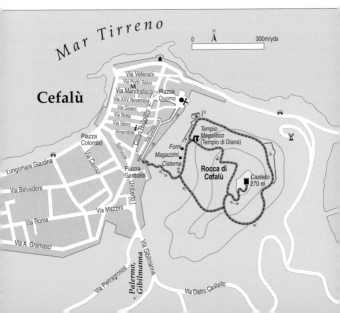

Walk 20: GIANT HOLLIES ON THE PIANO POMO

Distance: 3.5km/2.2mi; 1h45min

Grade: easy-moderate walk on nature trails and forestry tracks. Ascent and corresponding descent of 325m/1065ft

Equipment: hiking boots, food and water

How to get there and return: Shortly before the southern end of Castelbuono, leave the SS286 and turn right on the cul-de-sac road towards 'S. Giuglielmo ' and 'Rifugio Crispi' (Car tour 4). The road (the last section of which is poorly asphalted) ends after 11km on the Piano Sempria. 🚗 park at the Rifugio Francesco Crispi. You can eat and stay overnight in the Rifugio Crispi, tel.: 0921672279. Otherwise, a nice B&B near the old town of Castelbuono lies on the road to Isnello: Villa Letizia, Via Isnello, tel.: 0921673247.

Longer walk: After descending from the Cozzo Luminario to the Piano Imperiale, follow the cart track to the left. With the Croci dei Monticelli to your right, you cross pastures, curving gently uphill to the left. A wooden ladder helps you over a fence at the side of a locked gate (15min); the Croci are now behind you. At the junction immediately after, go left. This area, formerly grazed, has been reafforested with pines. The now-faint cart track runs through grass. After you pass a gate and a trough, the track reasserts itself. Once you have crossed the crest (25min), you have a good view to Monte Ferro and Pizzo Canna. Turn left here, on a path which rapidly descends beneath gnarled oaks and beech trees. In the valley between Pizzo Stefano and Monte Ferro, the path turns east. You pass a lone cottage and go through a gate, then meet a crossing gravel track (50min), which you follow to the left. The track runs through bushy pastures beneath the escarpment of Pizzo Stefano on the left. Turn left when you come to a concreted trough (1h05min) and, after a final ascent, you're back at the Piano Pomo (7km/4.3mi; 3h05min). Walk straight past the *pagghiaru* and through the gate, to where the waymarked nature trail branches off to the right. Return to the Rifugio Crispi along your outgoing route.

Ope of Sicily's great natural wonders awaits you on the Piano Pomo. More than 200 holly trees (*Ilex aquifolium*) stand together and form a magical grove. These trees, hundreds of years old, have grown to a colossal size and are unique in Italy. From November onwards, they are covered with shiny red berries.

The walk begins at the CLEARING at the **Piano Sempria** (1187m/3893ft). A signboard with a map shows the waymarked *Sentiero Natura* (nature trail), part of which you will follow on this walk. Turn right on the nature trail near the *rifugio,* climbing in zigzags through the woods. Butcher's broom (*Ruscus aculeatus*) and cyclamen form the undergrowth. The trail crosses the forestry track coming up from the Piano Sempria (**8min**). A giant 800-year-old downy oak stands beside the trail.

The path climbs higher, crosses a FIRE-BREAK and leads into an oak copse. Lichen hanging from the trees, and mossy rocks, make this woods a fairy-tale setting. You come to a CLEARING above the Vallone Canna (**15min**). To the south lies Monte S. Salvatore (Walk 21) and to the east you can make out Geraci Siculo, the Nebrodi and Mount Etna. The path now runs along the edge of the slope for a while. The wild rose bushes and holm oaks along here have been transformed by grazing cattle into a bizarre baroque garden. When the nature trail meets the forestry road again, follow it to the left, through the GATE and onto the **Piano Pomo** (1360m/4462ft; **35min**). An elongated *pagghiaru* stands on the pasture. In the past, these shelters built of stones and covered with rushes were built by the shepherds. This particular *pagghiaru* is a shelter for the forestry workers, and one of the rooms is always open for hikers.

With your back to the shelter, step over the FENCE and walk through the bracken over to the grove of hollies. Cross the grove until you reach a giant beech with the sign 'FAGGIO SECOLARE'. Here

Shepherds' hut on the Piano Pomo. This pagghiaru serves the forestry workers as a shelter and one of the rooms is always open for hikers.

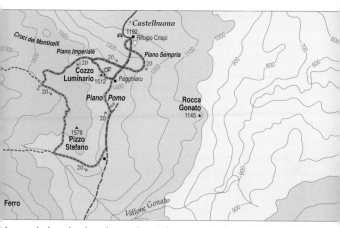

the path bends sharply to the right and climbs quickly under beeches. Passing moss-covered rocks, you head up left to the RIDGE and then the rocky PEAK of **Cozzo Luminario** (1512m/4959ft; **1h05min**). The panorama is spectacular, and the highest peaks of the Madonie surround you: Pizzo Carbonara (Walk 22) and Pizzo della Principessa to the west, Monte Ferro to the south. You can see down over Castelbuono and the Tyrrhenian Sea.

Descend north along the RIDGE and follow the path marked by wooden posts down to the **Piano Imperiale** (**1h10min**), a wide lime-stone valley. When you come to a crossing cart track (**1h15min**), follow it to the right *(but go left for the Longer walk)*. The track enters the beech wood and descends in zigzags. At the next JUNCTION (**1h25min**) there are two ways back down to the Piano Sempria: the steep forestry road to the left or the nature trail (a few minutes to the right). Both routes end at the **Rifugio Crispi** (**1h45min**).

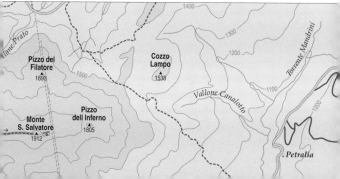

Walk 21: VALLONE MADONNA DEGLI ANGELI

See map pages 92-93   **Distance:** 8km/5mi; 2h20min

Grade: moderate walk on forestry tracks and narrow nature trails. Ascent and corresponding descent of 420m/1380ft

Equipment: hiking boots, sun protection, wind/waterproofs, food and water

How to get there and return: Drive from Polizzi Generosa on the SP119 towards 'Collesano' and 'Piano Battaglia'; 500m beyond the km8 road-marker, 🚗 park in front of the green iron gate of the forestry commission (Car tour 4). In Polizzi Generosa I recommend Ai Templari, Piazza Castello 7, tel.: 0921688173, www. ristoranteaitemplari.it — just five cosy rooms in an old castle, and great cuisine.

Longer walk: Before descending on the northern side of the Vallone Madonna degli Angeli, you can climb to the top of Monte S. Salvatore. When you reach the forestry track at the 1h25min-point, follow it uphill to the right. Soon afterwards you reach a saddle (1651m/5415ft). Continue further uphill to the right through low beech wood. The forestry track bends sharply to the left by a distinctive rock formation just above the weather station (15min). A gentle, drawn-out ascent follows, giving you time to enjoy the far-off view to the church of Madonna dell'Alto. Turn left at the next junction. The gravel track leads through an iron barrier (25min) and up to the antennas (40min). Follow the ridge to the east, to the trig point on Monte S. Salvatore (1912m/6270ft; 1h05min), with its fine panorama. Descend the same way (15km/9.3mi; 4h20min).

Magnificent mountain landscapes and botanical rarities await you on this walk. The woodlands of the Madonie range boast the largest number of species in the Mediterranean. Some plants *only* grow here — for example last specimens of the Nebrodi fir (*Abies nebrodensis*), which still survive in the Vallone Madonna degli Angeli and are extinct everywhere else. One of the most impressive mountain formations of the Madonie is the Quacella, which opens in a wide arc to the west. If you take the option of doing the longer walk up to Monte S. Salvatore, you will overlook most of the highest peaks in the Madonie and much of Sicily besides.

The walk begins at the GREEN IRON GATE (1240m/4068ft) of the forestry commission. A wooden ladder helps you to cross the FENCE. A weather station stands to the right. Follow the forestry track uphill. From the first switchback you have a clear view to the mountain arc of the Quacella. Further to the north lies the barren Pizzo Antenna. The gravel track bends south and continues rising. To the west you can see a low mountain tableland from which the Rocca Busambra (Walk 31) throws up its prominent peak. The track then bends to the left round a spur (**25min**).

As the track rises further, a deeply-etched valley accompanies you to the right. When the

View from the Vallone Madonna degli Angeli to the Cervi massif

forestry track bends left (1390m/4560ft; **30min**), continue straight ahead on a path (initially flanked by WOODEN RAILINGS).

Cross the floor of the **Vallone Madonna degli Angeli** (1370m/4495ft), where the last specimens of Nebrodi firs, relics of the Ice Age, can be found. You can recognise these beautiful conifers thanks to their vertically-poised, candle-like cones. The path ascends in zigzags once more, now passing some beautiful rock formations. After descending into the small valley of a tributary, the path rises under beech trees and then contours round a slope covered with debris. To the left you can see Monte Quacella and Monte Mufara. The path ascends in earnest once more, first through an oak grove, then a pine wood, until it meets the faint markings of a cart track. Follow this level track to the left. Another cart track, coming from Polizzi Generosa, joins you from the right. Continue to the left and leave the forest for a grass-covered limestone PLATEAU (1615m/5299ft; **1h15min**). A small weather station stands to the left. To the right you can see the pilgrims' church of Madonna dell'Alto about 2km away (as the crow flies).

Walk straight ahead on the gravel track, with the Vallone Madonna degli Angeli and Monte Quacella to your left. Ignoring a fork to the right, you reach a crossing forestry track (1635m/5364ft; **1h25min**). Turning right here, you could prolong the walk by ascending Monte S. Salvatore (Longer walk).

Now on the northern side of the Vallone degli Angeli, follow the forestry track downhill to the left. You pass a TROUGH and an isolated white house (**1h30min**). A wooden table and benches invite you to take a short break. The forestry track descends in deep hairpin bends, with beautiful views, and brings you back to the starting point at the GREEN IRON GATE (**2h20min**).

Walk 22: PIZZO CARBONARA

See map pages 92-93   **Distance:** 5.5km/3.4mi; 2h45min

Grade: moderate-strenuous walk along forestry tracks, footpaths and limestone terrain. Orientation is a problem if visibility is poor due to mist or fog. Ascent and corresponding descent of 380m/1245ft

Equipment: hiking boots, wind/waterproofs, food and water

How to get there and return: From the Portella Colla (Car tour 4) turn off to the Piano Battaglia. After the Ostello della Gioventù turn right on the one-way road and, at the next junction, turn left towards Piano Zucchi. 🚌 park after 200m, in front of the sign 'Piano Battaglia', where a wide gravel road branches off to the right. You can stay overnight and eat well at the restaurant Ai Templari in Polizzi Generosa (see Walk 21).

You will climb the highest peak of the Madonie in a fascinating limestone landscape. It has been found that the water which seeps into the basins of the Carbonara massif rises back to the surface as a spring at the foot of the Rocca di Cefalù. Great flocks of sheep are lead up to these high-altitude pastures in summer and autumn.

The walk begins at the wide limestone plain of the **Piano Battaglia** (1605m/5264ft). Thanks to the grazing animals, the grass is as short as a bowling green. With your back to wooded Monte Mufara, turn off the asphalted road onto the wide gravel road and, immediately afterwards, fork left on a field track. This track runs above the large basin, and you can see the **Inghiottitoio della Battaglietta**, a sink-hole, at the bottom of the hollow. The barren massif of Monte Ferro rises in front of you. As the track starts to rise in zigzags, a CHAIN BARRIER blocks vehicles. From a little meadow with a dilapidated STONE HOUSE on the left (1695m/5560ft; **20min**), follow the red spray-paint waymarks to the left into the beech wood. After 100 m/yds go left at the fork. Then the track makes a 90° turn to the left and rises across open terrain with good views to the surrounding mountains. The tracks curves to the right, leads back into the beech wood and passes a lichen-laden maple (1735m/5690ft; **30min**), then continues as a narrow zigzag path with some RED AND BLUE WAYMARKS. Back in the open, the cairned path curves right, above a series of sink-holes which gently descend to the foot of Pizzo Carbonara on your left. When you reach a small, deep SINK-HOLE on your right (**1h**), follow the RED FLASHES straight up to the RIDGE, then follow the SPINE to the right, to the stone pyramid marking the PEAK of **Pizzo Carbonara** (1979m/ 6491ft; **1h30min**), the second-highest mountain in Sicily. On a clear day the view reaches as far as the Aeolian Islands and Etna.

Descend the same way and continue down the RIDGE, following CAIRNS and BLUE FLASHES; the flat roof of the Rifugio del Carbonara is visible ahead. The sink-holes are now on your left. In the lowest hollow, you can just about make out the ruins of a dilapidated *ovile* (sheepfold). Crossing a little plain brings you to the unsupervised **Rifugio del Carbonara** (also called '**Bivacco Scolonazzo**' (1875m/ 6150ft; **2h**). It's just a short way up to the left — and the grave of the brave dog Argo, 'who possesed all the virtues of man, but none of his failings'.

Enjoy the views from the hilltop, then walk back down to the refuge (**2h10min**) and descend the path between WOODEN POSTS. Meet a crossing trail, waymarked with RED AND WHITE FLASHES, and follow this downhill to the left. You leave the beechwood and emerge in a CLEARING. The Cervi massif rises to the west, the little Lago Zucchi sits at your feet in the valley and, further in the north, you look out to the Gulf of Termini Imerese. Shortly afterwards the way forks (**2h25min**). The red- and white-waymarked route branches off to the right and meets the asphalt road in about 15 minutes, where you turn left for about 1km, back to your starting point.

However, if you have a clear day, go *straight ahead* at this junction, towards the Rifugio Marini. Head towards Monte Mufara, until you can see the houses on the Piano Battaglia below you. There is no clear path, so just make your own way back down to your car at the **Piano Battaglia** (**2h45min**).

In the Madonie: Cork oaks (Quercus suber) near Geraci Siculo (top); harvesting olives near Castelbuono (right); the Piano Battaglia (below).

Walk 23: GANGIVECCHIO AND MONTE ZIMMARA

Distance: 6.5km/4mi; 2h20min

Grade: easy-moderate walk, only a bit steep on the initial part of the ascent. Gravel roads and small country tracks. Ascent and corresponding descent of 450m/1475ft

Equipment: hiking boots, sun and wind protection, spare layers, food and water

How to get there and return: At the western edge of Gangi (Car tour 4), turn off the SS120 towards Gangivecchio and after 4.5km 🚗 park in front of the Masseria Gangivecchio. The Tenuta Gangivecchio, a former abbey, used to be my recommended hotel-restaurant in this area, but unfortunately it was about to close at press date. Instead, I now suggest Casale Villa Rainò (Contrada Rainò, tel.: 0921644680, www.villaraino.it), an old manor house 4km outside Gangi. The owner, Aldo Conte, knows a lot about hiking in the area.

Longer walk: From the 2h05min-point at the watering place, follow the asphalt road a short while. Before it reaches the hilltop, turn left on the gravel track (where a barrier blocks vehicle access). Further uphill, ignore a track off left to the Masseria Soprano; keep straight ahead. Go round another vehicle barrier and, shortly after the hilltop (960m/3148ft; 20min), turn left through a gate. The track leads across meadows, goes through two more gates and heads right, up to a plateau, the Balza di Pezzolunga (1055m/3460ft; 45min). In antiquity this was a fortified acropolis; today it still offers wide views all around. Return the same way and continue the main walk (adds 3km/2mi; 1h20min).

Monte Zimmara is the highest elevation between the Madonie and Nebrodi and so offers excellent views. But despite its listed status in the Mediterranean bio-geographical region, the State electricity company has erected a wind farm on the ridge! The Masseria Gangivecchio is set in rural and peaceful surroundings, a nice place to break a car tour or relax at the end of the walk.

The walk begins at the **Masseria Gangivecchio** (831m/2726ft). Follow the asphalt road east for a short way and cross the **Torrente Capuano**. Shortly after the BRIDGE, turn left on a cobbled road (**5min**). The cobbles give way to gravel, as the road climbs steeply south, passing solitary houses, vineyards and a small oak grove. After a while fields and pastureland take over, while the Madonie Mountains appear to the right. Without branching off, the ascent continues more gently. After passing a large farmhouse built around a courtyard, you cross the asphalt road. Keep climbing on the newly laid cobbled road. Past a STABLE, the road bends right to a car park

Near Gangivecchio

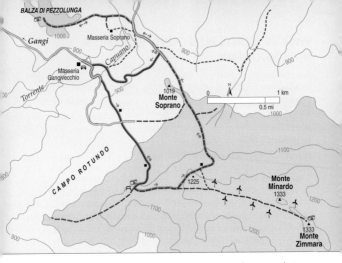

(1080m/3543ft; **50min**). From here you enjoy an unobstructed view to the Madonie and Gangi. The houses of Gangi (photograph page 26) cluster like sheep on the tilting plateau. Down in the valley you can see the buildings of the Masseria Gangivecchio, surrounded by trees and hazelnut groves.

When you come to a fenced-in PICNIC AREA, follow the gravel track as it swings left along the RIDGE. The track runs through a gate and uphill between fences. To the right lie afforested areas, whereas rock-covered pastures are to the left. The track now rises with the ridge and leads between wind turbines towards the top of Monte Zimmara. This 1333m-high peak used to be one of the highlights of this walk, but if you dislike the turbines as much as I do, you will *leave* the gravel track when you come to a level cart track diverting to the left (1135m/3724ft; **1h**).

Keeping the ridge with the wind turbines to your right, descend the faint, hardly-used cart track past a SHEPHERDS' HUT and a SHEEP-FOLD. Deeply eroded, the track then bends left and leads down to a WATERING PLACE (**1h30min**). By now the track is clearly defined; it follows the RIDGE between fenced-in fields and pastures. Remains of old cobbles can still be seen underfoot. Without leaving the SPINE OF THE RIDGE, continue straight ahead downhill, ignoring a wider track turning off to the right. With wide views of inland Sicily and Mount Etna in the east, the route leads east round **Monte Soprano**. Your surroundings alternate between little orchards, vineyards and a grove of aspens. Beyond a SADDLE, and with views to the Masseria Soprano, the track descends to a narrow asphalted road (**2h**).

Follow the road a short while towards the Masseria Soprano; then, when you come to a WATERING PLACE (895m/2937ft; **2h05min**), turn sharp left on a gravel road. After passing hazelnut groves and a downy oak wood (*Quercus pubescens*), you cross the Capuano again. Beyond a couple of houses, you reach the asphalt road that takes you quickly back to the **Masseria Gangivecchio** (**2h20min**).

99

Walk 24: MONTE PELLEGRINO, PALERMO'S HOLY MOUNTAIN

See photograph page 49

Distance: 9km/5.6mi; 3h10min

Grade: moderate walk, with a steep ascent through the Vallone del Porco. Nature trails, forestry tracks, a short stretch on an asphalt road and stone-paved steps (slippery after rain!). Ascent of 430m/1345ft, descent of 465m/1526ft

Equipment: hiking boots, food and water

How to get there and return: In Palermo take AMAT (www.amat.pa.it) 🚌 806 from Piazza Sturzo behind the Teatro Politeama towards Mondello (Car tours 5, 6). Get off in the Parco della Favorita at the Ex Scuderie Reali/Casa natura. (A visitors' centre is a little further ahead on Viale Diana; www.riservamonte pellegrino.palermo.it). At the end of the walk return from Via Martin Luther King on AMAT 🚌 812 to the town centre (there is also a bus stop below the sanctuary of S. Rosalia). Tickets for the AMAT buses are available in bars and tobacconists, but *not* on the buses themselves. There is a wide choice of hotels in Palermo. A recommended hotel in the centre is: Letizia, Via Bottai 30, tel.: 091589110, www.hotelletizia.com.

Alternative walk: From Via Martin Luther King the old cobbled pilgrims' trail leads up to the sanctuary of S. Rosalia. Walk up and back down the same way.

Monte Pellegrino seems to exercise a general fascination. For Goethe it was the 'most beautiful promontory in the world', for both the Palermitans and (interestingly) the Tamils living in Palermo, Pellegrino is a 'holy mountain'. The mountain's many limestone caves attracted people even back in the Stone Age. In the Archaeological Museum in Palermo you can see the casts of palaeolithic stone engravings from the Grotta dell'Addaura. During the 12th century, Rosalia di Sinibaldo lived as an hermit in one of these caves. After she managed (posthumously) to free Palermo of the plague, she was chosen as the city's patron saint and is still celebrated every July with boisterous festivities.

The walk begins at the BUS STOP at the **Ex Scuderie Reali** (75m/ 246ft). Turn right into the lane which leads directly to the deeply-etched valley, past the round tower (formerly a powder magazine; 86m/282ft). To the right are the Ex Scuderie Reali, the former Royal Stables of the Bourbons, today a natural history centre. The steep limestone rock walls of Monte Pellegrino rise in front of you. Climbing the narrow winding path up the **Vallone del Porco**, you quickly leave the town and its noise behind. Typical species of the Mediterranean maquis — especially lime-loving plants like the Judas tree (*Cercis siliquastrum*) — grow between the boulders.

After a first steep section, the path rises more gently in the shade of pines and eucalyptus trees (**35min**). Lined by stones, the path then leads to a DILAPIDATED BUILDING (385m/1263ft; **50min**). Go straight ahead, even if there is no clear path, until you meet a crossing asphalt road a few minutes later. Turn right and follow the road to a junction (410m/1345ft; **1h**). The walk will continue on the road to the left here but, first, cross to the car park surrounded by bars and hot-dog stands, then take steps up to the cave-shrine of **S. Rosalia** (425m/1394ft; **1h05min**).

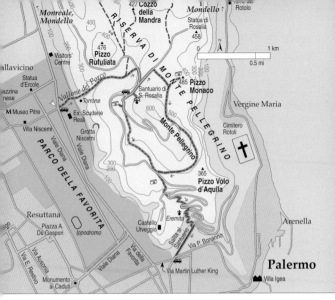

Return to the 1h-point at the crossing* and take Via Padre G. Casini, now on your *right*. After a few minutes, at an INFORMATION BOARD/MAP (425m/1394ft; **1h15min**), turn right on the broad trail rising in the shadow of pines, then follow the sign 'PIZZO MONACO' to the left. Rounded bushes of tree spurge *(Euphorbia dendroides)* contrast charmingly with the bare rock boulders forming the peak of **Pizzo Monaco** (485m/1591ft; **1h30min**). The view reaches from Capo Gallo in the west to Capo Zafferano in the east. On a clear day, you can even see the island of Ustica.

Back on the main route, turn left. After a few paces the path, now lined by stones, continues to the right. Then it rises in zigzags and meets an asphalt road (545m/1788ft; **2h**). Follow this to the left for just 5m/yds, then continue on the red-waymarked trail descending to the left — with views to Capo Zafferano. The old mule track curves to the right and meets a gravelled forestry track. Turn right here, now with fine views to the Castello Utvegio, Palermo and the surrounding mountains.

Once you have reached the old cobbled pilgrims' trail (345m/1132ft; **2h30min**), descend to the left with more good views of Palermo and the plain of Conca d'Oro (photograph page 49). On the way down, you cross the asphalt road several times — the real 'pilgrimage road' for the religious (but motorised) Palermitans. When the road was closed temporarily after a landslide, the number of the pilgrims declined remarkably! The old trail ends on **Via Martin Luther King** (40m/131ft; **3h10min**).

---

*Or, to shorten the walk and return from S. Rosalia, you could either take bus 312 back to Palermo, or descend the cobbled pilgrims' trail. From the bottom of the steps, follow the asphalt road to the left and, after just a few paces, turn left uphill on Via al Santuario. From the highest point of this road keep straight ahead. The cobbled trail will end eventually on Via Martin Luther King.

Walk 25: THE CASTELLACCIO ON PIZZO DEL CORVO

Distance: 2km/1.2mi; 50min
Grade: easy walk on nature trails. Ascent and corresponding descent of 180m/590ft
Equipment: lightweight hiking boots, food and water

How to get there and return: 🚗 park at the Portella San Martino, a saddle between San Martino delle Scale and Monreale (Car tour 5). Regular No 2 Giordano 🚌 between Monreale/Via Agrigento and San Martino (www. autoservizigiordano.it). Ample accommodation in Palermo (see Walk 24).

The castle on Pizzo del Corvo was built in the 12th century to protect the monastery in Monreale. The view from the peak over the Conca d'Oro is unique — ideal for a picnic!

The walk begins at the SADDLE at the **Portella S. Martino** (595m/1952ft). Steps (cobbled at the outset) lead up to the clearly-visible castle. The CAS (Sicilian Alpine Club) maintains the walk and opens the castle to the public on Sundays and holidays from 09.00-17.00. On the ascent the Benedictine abbey at San Martino is visible to the left. It's a straightforward climb to the CASTLE on the PEAK of **Pizzo del Corvo** (also called Monte Caputo; 776m/2545ft; **20min**). Follow the path clockwise round the castle; a group of rocks on the southeast side is a perfect picnic spot (**25min**). Savour the view: the entire Conca d'Oro plain, with Palermo and the sea, spreads in front of you.

To return, walk a short way north from the castle (with the car park on your left), until you meet the partly overgrown, old cobbled trail. (If in doubt, retrace your steps.) As you descend to the right, the path will become more clear. Once out of the pines, you look down on the imposing monastery in Monreale. The path bends right and descends in zigzags. Back on asphalt, turn right for 400m/yds, to the **Portella S. Martino** (**50min**).

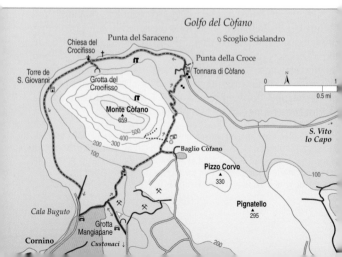

Walk 26: MONTE COFANO

See map opposite, below **Distance:** 8km/5mi; 2h45min

Grade: moderate walk on signposted nature trails. Pleasant beaches en route, but no shade. Ascent and corresponding descent of 250m/820ft

Equipment: hiking boots, sun protection, swimming things, food and water

How to get there and return: 🚍 park at the Grotta Mangiapane (Car tour 5) — or (more easily) on Lungomare C. Colombo in Cornino (the 2h33min-point in the walk). Most of the restaurants here only open in summer. Accommodation in the family-run Albergo-Ristorante Il Cortile in Custonaci (Via Scurati 67, tel.: 0923971750, www.hotelilcortile.it); the owner is an expert on the area!

Notes: The Grotta Mangiapane opens daily from 08.00-12.00 and from 15.00-17.00; there are toilets. In summer the Torre della Tonnara di Cofano (1h25min-point) opens for visitors as well.

The majestic silhouette of Monte Còfano (659m/2162ft) is a striking headland on the Sicilian coast. It's a spectacular limestone outcrop, protected as an nature reserve and harbours more than 325 plant species, many of them endemic or rare. The area is rich in prehistoric caves — one of which, the Grotta Mangiapane, shelters a tiny hamlet, complete with stone-built houses and stables! The mountains around Custonaci are one of Italy's most important marble-cutting centres.

The walk starts at the **Grotta Mangiapane** (60m/197ft): continue north on the broad gravel road. At the next crossing (50m/164ft; **5min**) take the gravel track rising to your right, with Monte Còfano in full view ahead. Huge stone blocks lie on the ground like Cyclops' toys, while the white cliffs of partly-abandoned QUARRIES tower overhead. The Gulf of Bonagia opens up to your left, with Levanzo (Walk 28) further to the west. The track, narrower now, circles behind a LOW BUILDING and zigzags up the rocky slope.

Shortly before reaching the saddle, a path joins from the right. Follow the sign 'TONNARA DI COFANO' to the left. From the SADDLE (250m/820ft; **50min**) you overlook a small karst lake in a depression to the right and, hidden behind the rocky ridge, the hamlet of Baglio Còfano. Another path crosses here: left leads up Monte Còfano, but I wouldn't recommend it even for experienced climbers except in the company of a local guide; the rock is very friable. In any case, there is no need to climb to the top, since from the saddle there is a breathtaking panorama over the Còfano Gulf. In the northeast Monte Monaco dominates the seaside resort of San Vito lo Capo, and to the east, behind the Monte del Passo di Lupo and Monte Speziale chain, lie the turquoise coves of Zingaro (Walk 27).

Accompanied by these views, the old mule track descends in wide arcs. Dwarf fan palms and tufts of Mauritanian grass have taken the place of vineyards, orchards and fields of grain on the abandoned agricultural terraces. A massive WATCHTOWER (open for visitors in summer) appears above the sea, built in the 17th century to protect the *tonnara* (fish processing plant) from Turkish invasions. Past a couple of ruins, the clear path swings left, still descending in hairpins, eventually at the left of a wall topped with barbed wire.

Monte Còfano from Erice

The **Tonnara di Còfano** (10m/33ft; **1h25min**) today harbours romantic holiday apartments. The pebble coves below the watchtower are good swimming spots when the sea is calm. Virgil recounts in his *Aeneid* how Aeneas organised funeral games on this shore to honour his late father, among others a boat race to the rock jutting out of the sea, the **Scoglio Scialandro** of today.

Follow the track 200m/yds north, where it gives way to a clear path on the left. Rugged limestone projects into the sea; dwarf fan palms, pungent wild thyme and thistles cover the lower slopes of Monte Còfano. Sheer cliffs loom up ahead — home to peregrine falcons and Bonelli's eagles. A solitary fig tree shelters a rock-hewn SHRINE TO S. NICOLA DI BARI (30m/98ft; **2h**), patron saint of fishermen and sailors. The shrine announces the chapel a few minutes further on. From this **Chiesa del Crocifisso** (45m/148ft; **2h05min**) a short detour leads up to the **Grotta del Crocefisso** (55m/180ft; **2h10min**), which has provided a wealth of prehistoric archeological findings.

Back at the chapel, continue west towards 'TORRE SARACENA'. The vegetation is lusher now; abandoned terraces on the slopes tell of former cultivation. While the watchtower rises ahead of you, your view stretches to Mount Erice and across the Gulf of Bonagia to the Egadi Islands in the west. Steps take you up to the watchtower, the **Torre di S. Giovanni** (35m/115ft; **2h20min**). If you climb to the top, beware of the (hopefully) covered cistern-hole in the entrance!

Beyond the tower, dwarf fan palms form a waist-high thicket, but the pasturing cows seem even more exotic in this landscape. Approaching Lido Cornino, you pass humble old fishermens' houses and some newly built villas. Turn right on Via Alassio, down to the beach in **Cornino** (5m/16ft; **2h30min**). Follow asphalted Lungomare C. Colombo a few hundred metres/yards to the left, to a crossroads (10m/33ft; **2h33min**) with a nature reserve INFORMATION BOARD/MAP. From here take the broad gravel road up to the left. The next crossing is the 5min-point of your outgoing walk. Turn right, back to the **Grotta Mangiapane** (**2h45min**).

Walk 27: THE ZINGARO NATURE RESERVE

NB: No dogs allowed!   **Distance:** 15km/9.3mi; 5h20min

Grade: moderate-strenuous walk on well-built nature trails. Pleasant beaches en route, but no shade. Ascent and corresponding descent of 600m/1970ft

Equipment: hiking boots, sun protection, swimming things, food and water

How to get there and return: 🚌 park at the southern entrance to the Parco dello Zingaro. There are some small hotels in Scopello (Car tour 5), a small village to the south of the nature reserve, among them the excellent Pensione Tranchina, Via Armando Diaz 7, tel.: 0924541099, www.pensionetranchina.com.

**Shorter walks (*Note:* a fee is charged for visiting the reserve (www.riservazingaro.it, but it is worth it as it includes the museums and a free 1:25,000 trail map.)

1 The main trail in the reserve runs parallel with the coast and is waymarked. You can follow this from the southern park entrance to the Tonarella dell'Uzzo. Then continue along the beach and arc back to the Grotta dell'Uzzo. From here retrace your steps back to the southern entrance (11km/6.8mi; 3h).

2   Follow the main trail parallel with the coast to the Grotta dell'Uzzo. After visiting the cave, retrace your steps a short way, then go up to the Contrada Sughero. Return to the southern entrance to the nature reserve via Pizzo del Corvo (11km/6.8mi; 3h15min).

Majestic limestone mountains, gorgeous turquoise-blue bays and a subtropical vegetation with dwarf fan palms are among the natural wonders of the Zingaro Nature Reserve. A successful citizens' protest in 1980 prevented the authorities from building a coastal road here, and so Sicily's first nature reserve was born. This example led to the creation of almost 100 more nature reserves and three large regional parks (the Sicilian equivalent of national parks).

The walk begins at the CAR PARK at the **southern entrance** (85m/279ft) to the Parco dello Zingaro. A gravel road leads through a TUNNEL and then becomes a clear path; follow the signs 'CENTRO VISITATORI' to the left. There is a little natural history museum and toilet in the **Visitors' Centre** (65m/213ft; **15min**). Just above the centre, take the path signposted 'PIZZO DEL CORVO', zigzagging up the open slope to your left. You overlook the Gulf of Castellamare in the east, while the wide ridge of Pizzo Passo del Lupo rises in front of you. Meeting a track (where a BLACK IRON GATE is to the left; 260m/853ft; **45min**), turn right on the track. It ends in front of a little house further to the north (**50min**).

Turn left here, on a narrow path leading diagonally up the slope. On the ascent, the path forks (305m/1001ft; **55min**). While it is possible to go left here up to Pianello, keep right on the main route, and cross the floor of a valley. Ignore the next faint turn-off to the left, and you will reach a small plateau. The path leads across a SADDLE between Pizzo Passo del Lupo and Pizzo del Corvo. Make a short detour to the right here, to **Pizzo del Corvo** (403m/1322ft; **1h25min**). Your reward is a magnificent view: Monte Inici rises to the south, behind Scopello, the Gulf of Castellamare runs off to the west, and the Parco dello Zingaro, with its innumerable turquoise-blue bays, spreads out in front of you. To the north you can see the Contrada Sughero and the Baglio Cosenza, two abandoned settlements you will pass on this walk.

Follow the main path, heading north, and descend towards the houses of Sughero, crossing two valleys. The way through the **Contrada Sughero** leads past abandoned almond and olive groves. The path diverting to the right here descends to the coast trail (255m/837ft; **2h10min**). When you reach the last, most northerly house (**2h15min**), take the path climbing up to the left in zigzags. The path leads over a PASS and, after crossing a sloping plateau, reaches the **Baglio Cusenza** (450m/1476ft; **2h50min**), the HIGHEST POINT of this walk. The houses of the Baglio were abandoned in the 1960s; only the pastures are still frequented by cattle and sheep. The limestone landscape is rough and wild — almost Nordic in appearance.

From the Baglio follow the cart track north, to the valley

Dwarf fan palms (Chamaerops humilis), the emblem of the Zingaro Nature Reserve, flourish near the coast, while on the bare limestone slopes, grass (Ampelodesmus mauretanica), asphodels (Asphodelus aestivus) and wild fennel find a foothold. Rosemary bushes give off their unmistakable aroma. Spring and late autumn transform this landscape into a veritable sea of colourful blooms.

(465m/1526ft; **3h05min**). Turn right on the path along the valley floor, down into the Contrada Uzzo. Along the way you pass the opening of the **Grotta Mastro Peppe Siino**. The vegetation grows more abundant now, and dwarf fan palms again appear. The path describes a wide arc to the right and bends south, with the richly-indented coast of the reserve in front of you. When you come to a crossing path (45m/148ft; **3h45min**), follow it to the right. The Contrada Uzzo is like a green oasis. The almond grove is surrounded by a lush thicket of dwarf fan palms. The Grotta dell'Uzzo lies ahead. The path forks in the valley below the cave (**3h55min**). Just a few minutes downhill to the left is the Cala dell'Uzzo, one of the most beautiful coves in Sicily.

Passing the **Grotta dell'Uzzo,** follow the main trail, parallel with the coast, back to the southern entrance to the park. This part of the walk is especially lovely and varied, and along the undulating way you can descend to one of the many solitary bays for another swim. A particularly beautiful spot is the **Contrada Zingaro** (40m/131ft; **4h25min**), where the dwarf fan palms which symbolise the reserve flourish in luxuriant abundance. Shortly before the park exit you pass below the **Centro Visitatori** (**5h10min**). A path branching off left here leads down to Cala della Capreria, another lovely bay. The main trail leads above the picnic area and through a tunnel, back to the CAR PARK (**5h20min**).

Walk 28: STONE AGE PAINTINGS ON LEVANZO

Distance: 9km/5.6mi; 3h10min

Grade: easy-moderate walk on gravel tracks and well-built paths, although the short stretch to the Grotta del Genovese leads over somewhat rougher ground. Ascent and corresponding descent of 400m/1310ft

Equipment: hiking boots, sun protection, swimming things, food and water

How to get there and return: From Trapani (Car tour 5) by ⛴ ferry or hydrofoil. Several connections daily (schedules are printed in the daily papers). There are two simple hotels on Levanzo, and hotels of various categories in Trapani. I recommend the well-kept B&B Al Lumi in the old town, Corso V. Emanuele 71, tel.: 0923540922, www.ailumi.it.

Note: If you want to see the Stone Age paintings in the Grotta del Genovese, contact the custodian on Levanzo in advance: Natale Castiglione, Via Lungomare 27, tel.: 0923924032, mobile: 3397418800, www.grottadelgenovese.it.

Levanzo, the smallest of the Egadi Islands, is studded with limestone caves, in which people have sought refuge since the Stone Age. Important wall paintings and incised drawings from this early phase of the history of mankind are preserved in the Grotta del Genovese. Amazingly, the islanders only left the caves in the 19th century, to move to the houses around the little port.

The walk begins at the PORT at **Cala Dogana**. A road (only asphalted for a short way) runs from the port straight across the island to Capo Grosso. Follow this road for about 1.5km/1mi. The road rises steeply in the village of Levanzo, then flattens out and crosses a cultivated plateau. The ridge which culminates in Pizzo del Monaco rises in the west. At the **Case Tramontana** turn left on a gravel track (**30min**). This track then bends to the right and runs between drystone walls. After a short while, turn left on a path, which leads past the **Rifugio Forestale**, where a pine plantation begins (**40min**). Walk through a gap in the wall, and climb the zigzag path up left to the peak of **Pizzo del Monaco** (278m/912ft; **1h05min**), for the fine views.

Then return to the main path (**1h25min**) and continue west. Cala Tramontana and Capo Grosso (with the lighthouse) lie to the right. As the path descends, the jagged silhouette of Marettimo appears. At the point where the path bends south and a drystone wall runs down to the sea, you begin your descent to the Grotta del Genovese (**1h30min**). The entrance to the cave lies at Punta del Genovese, a limestone rock rising dramatically by the shore. The narrow path descends in zigzags to the little bay and then runs along to the cave. The remains of a limekiln can be seen in the foyer of the cave. The **Grotta del Genovese** itself is locked and can be visited only in company of the custodian after the entrance fee is paid (see 'Note' above).

Return the same way back to the main trail (**2h**). The path continues along the western foothills of Pizzo del Monaco. Behind a light stand of pines, the path starts to descend a terraced slope, down to an abandoned settlement (**2h30min**), where you'll see some cisterns. Since there aren't any natural springs on Levanzo,

In the Grotta del Genovese

the water had to be collected from the bare rock faces and stored in these cisterns. Behind the last farmstead the path leads through a WOODEN GATE and bends toward the sea. Descending via rock-cut steps, the path then veers left. The snow-white limestone rocks along the coast and the bright yellow tree spurge *(Euphorbia dendroides)* contrast strikingly. The path descends further until, when you are opposite the **Faraglione Islands**, a few steps lead you to a little pebble beach (**2h50min**). Have a refreshing swim in this clear water, then follow the narrow asphalted road back to the PORT at **Cala Dogana** (**3h10min**).

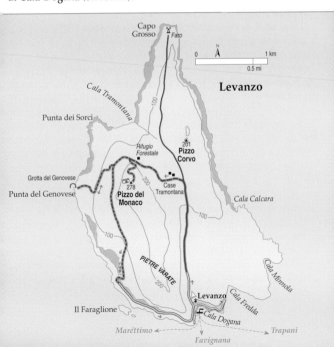

Walk 29: LA PIZZUTA

Distance: 9km/5.6mi; 4h
Grade: moderate-strenous, with some steep ascents on gravel roads; otherwise nature trails. The return path is slippery and overgrown in places. Ascent and corresponding descent of 550m/1804ft. After the 2h10min-point the path is very overgrown due to lack of maintenance. Only adventurous hikers should carry on from this point — easier in spring and late autumn, and secateurs would come in handy!
Equipment: hiking boots, sun protection, windproofs, water
How to get there and return: Leave Piana degli Albanesi (Car tour 6) on the SP34 towards 'SS624 Palermo–Sciacca'. At the southwestern edge of town take a sharp right, following the sign 'Percorso N° 17: Piana d. A. — Pizzuta'. 🚗 park below the Chiesa dell'Odigitria. The little church can also be reached in 15min on foot from the main street in Piana centre by following the red/white SI (Sentiero Italia) signposting uphill. Piana degli Albanesi is regularly served on weekdays by Prestia & Comandè buses from Palermo's Stazione Centrale. The *agriturismo* Sant'Agata, an impressive manor house, lies 9km east of Piana on the road to Ficuzza–Corleone (Contrada Sant'Agata, mobile: 3336707126 or 3384598654, www.santagatagriturismo.it).
Photograph: La Pizzuta

Rugged La Pizzuta stands out clearly in Palermo's hinterland. It offers great views over the Conca d'Oro and the capital. The area's *niviere* (snow pits) were used to store ice, which was then transported to Palermo in summer for the refreshment of the nobility in form of *granite* (sorbets). Piana degli Albanesi was founded in the end of the 15th century by Albanians fleeing Turkish domination. To this day the inhabitants preserve their language and Greek Orthodox rites, especially alive at Easter.

The walk begins at the **Chiesa dell'Odigitria** (785m/2575ft); there's a TRAIL MAP here covering the Riserva Naturale Orientata Serre della Pizzuta. Red/white SI waymarks and abundant signs guide you up the steep asphalted road, later a gravel track. Fields, orchards and broom cover the lower slopes of La Pizzuta, followed by vestiges of mixed oak woods, then pine plantations topped by crags. Shortly before the saddle, a waymarked path to the left leads to the limestone cave Grotta del Garrone; keep straight ahead. From the saddle, **Portella Garrone** (1150m/3773ft; **40min**), the view opens out to wild mountain scenery and vast pastures in the west and the Conca d'Oro to the north, with Monreale and Palermo on the sea.

While Mauritanian grass (*Amphelodesmos mauritanica*) grows in abundance, waymarks become scarce! The official SI (Sentiero Italia) crosses the valley basin to the west. The path becomes clear once again, running through low shrubs. After going through a GATE (975m/3199ft; **1h05min**) at the left of a rock outcrop, look out for a tile-clad house to the right. Head down to the narrow gravel road beside the house and follow it to the left. After a few minutes you

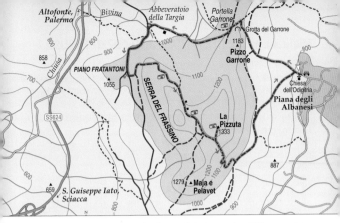

reach a crossing (920m/3018ft; **1h15min**) above the **Abbeveratoio della Targia**, a fountain with fresh drinking water.

Follow the steep gravel road uphill, passing the GREEN IRON GATE of the Demanio Forestale. The roads forks on a plateau with a huge WATER TANK, the **Piano Fratantoni** (1018m/3340ft; **1h45min**). Walk left towards 'PORTELLA DELLA GINESTRA', but after just a few steps turn off left on a trail rising in the shade of pines and cypresses. After five minutes you meet another gravel road, where you turn left. As this gravel road circles the **Serra del Frassino** clockwise to the left, the view opens up again to the Conca d'Oro. At the next junction (1120m/3675ft; **2h10min**) go straight ahead. Ruins and circular stone walls (the snow pits) in the **Valle delle Niviere** to the left catch the eye. Drawing level with the highest of the ruins (1215m/3986ft; **2h30min**), step over the low fence on your left. Then cross the pasture, heading uphill to the right. At the SADDLE (1225m/ 4019ft; **2h25min**), with a fine view to Monte Iato (site of antique Iaetas) and the Gulf of Castellamare, the path heads left over slabs of rock.

From the next SADDLE, between La Pizzuta and Maja e Pelavet (**2h35min**), make the short ascent to the peak. Follow the ridge to the left. There is some easy rock-climbing involved. On a clear day, the view from the SUMMIT OF **La Pizzuta** (1333m/4373ft; **2h50min**) takes in majestic Rocca Busambra (Walk 31) and Mount Etna.

On the return, zigzag down to the lowest point of the saddle, where a METAL SIGN (1220m/4003ft; **3h20min**) and FADED RED FLASHES on the rock mark the start of the old mule track. Descending back to Piana degli Albanesi, don't let the views distract you; keep your eyes on the trail (with the odd green/yellow wooden marker pole). The *mulattiera* zigzags down the southeastern slope of La Pizzuta, then enters a pine plantation, bends north and crosses a firebreak via a GATE (1020m/3346ft; **3h30min**). The broad trail passes through a SECOND GATE to the right, now running parallel with the firebreak to the north. Two minutes later you leave the fenced-in area through the next GATE (935m/3068ft; **3h40min**) to the right, where a wooden sign indicates the 'PERCORSO N° 17'. The trail eventually runs in the shadow of oaks, then broadens and passes the first buildings, paddocks and orchards before the **Chiesa dell'Odigitria** (**4h**).

111

Walk 30: VALLE DEL FANUSO AND COZZO FANUSO

Distance: 7.5km/4.7mi; 2h30min

Grade: moderate walk along forestry tracks and nature trails; the descent in the Valle Fanuso follows partly-overgrown cattle trails (secateurs would come in handy!) Ascent and corresponding descent of 260m/853ft

Equipment: hiking boots, food, water bottle (there are watering places en route)

How to get there and return: Following the road signs from Ficuzza (Car tour 6), after 5km you reach the mountain inn, Rifugio Alpe Cucco: 🚗 park here. You can eat well and stay overnight here, too, tel.: 0918208225, www. alpecucco.it. See also Walk 31.

There's an enchanted landscape awaiting discovery at the foot of Rocca Busambra. You wander in the shade of gnarled old oak trees and across sunlit meadows. The wood (Bosco della Ficuzza)

Paeonies in the Bosco della Ficuzza

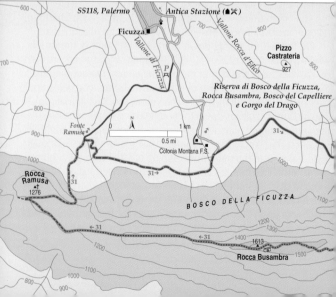

is at its most beautiful in April and May, when the peonies *(Paeonia mascula)* are in bloom. The sandstone cliffs of Cozzo Tondo will offer you wide-ranging views.

The walk begins at the **Rifugio Alpe Cucco** (945m/3100ft). Just east of the inn, the gravel road forks: head uphill to the right, towards Mezzojuso, passing a WATERING PLACE. The limestone rock walls of Rocca Busambra rise to your right, with the green oak woods surging up against it from below. The road leads through a light mixed deciduous wood, where cattle graze. Stay on the main gravel road until you are just a short way below the rounded brow of the ridge (1055m/3461ft; **50min**).

Then follow the signs 'SENTIERO CHIANU PRAINU' and 'FANUSO' to the left; go through a GATE and cross the pasture, heading into the oak wood. The broad track ends at a SADDLE (1015m/3330ft; **1h**), a crossroad of trails. To the right leads to the Valle Cerasa, whereas the trail to the left descends into the Valle del Fanuso (where you will continue the walk later). But first go straight on, into the man-made gap in the sandstone formation in front of you. The path initially follows the ridge, then runs into an old *mulattiera*, which rises in zigzags. At the next junction turn right for the final ascent to the SUMMIT OF **Cozzo Fanuso** (1078m/3537ft; **1h10min**). Cross over to the group of sandstone boulders above the Valle Cerasa, a wonderful resting place when it's not windy. The views are fantastic!

Return to the 1h10min-point at the SADDLE (**1h20min**) and descend to the right. Sparse green-yellow wooden poles mark the partly-overgrown path. Once at the bottom of the **Valle del Fanuso** (920m/3018ft; **1h35min**), cross the stream to your left. With your back to a dilapidated house, descend across open meadows. At the basin's deepest point you cross the stream again via a FORD. Following the course of the valley and going through TWO GATES,

you meet a wide forestry track (820m/2690ft; **2h**). Follow this uphill to the left; along the way more tracks join yours. Little by little, Godrano appears over the treetops, then Rocca Busambra, and finally the buildings of the Rifugio Alpe Cucco. The forestry track leads through a GREEN IRON GATE and meets the gravel road coming up from the Vallone d'Agnese. Walk straight ahead for a few minutes, back to the junction east of the **Rifugio Alpe Cucco** (**2h30min**).

Walk 31: ROCCA BUSAMBRA AND THE BOSCO DELLA FICUZZA

See map pages 112-113   **Distance:** 14km/8.7mi; 6h10min

Grade: strenuous and only recommended for experienced mountain walkers: there is no clear path along the steep crest of Rocca Busambra. If fog or mist develops, turn back. Otherwise the walk follows gravel tracks and good trails. Ascent and corresponding descent of 670m/2200ft

Equipment: hiking boots, sun/wind protection, spare layers, food and water

How to get there and return: as Walk 30, page 112

Shorter walk: There are plenty of walking possibilities in the Bosco della Ficuzza. You can get valuable advice in the Antica Stazione di Ficuzza in Ficuzza (tel.: 0918460000, www.anticastazione.it) — it's also a perfect place to eat and sleep!

A royal wood, the Bocca della Ficuzza, and a majestic mountain, Rocca Busambra, are the highlights of this walk. Hunting was the great passion of the Bourbon King Ferdinand IV, and he made sure that the forests were protected from further wood-cutting by establishing a *Real Riserva*. In 1803 his architect, Marvuglia, built the hunting castle in Ficuzza. Today this beautiful area is a protected nature reserve. Rocca Busambra itself is one of the most impressive mountain formations in Sicily, and the view from the top is magnificent, but the ascent does require some alpine mountaineering experience.

The walk begins at the **Rifugio Alpe Cucco** (945m/3100ft). Just east of the inn, the gravel road forks: head uphill to the right, towards Mezzojuso, passing a WATERING PLACE (**5min**) and entering a mixed oak wood. Follow the main gravel road, continuing uphill. The sandstone rocks of Cozzo Fanuso rise to your left, and in the west is the steep escarpment of Rocca Busambra. The road crosses an elongated CLEARING, passes the turn-off for Walk 30 (1055m) and leads over the ROUNDED BROW OF THE RIDGE (1070m/3510ft; **50min**). Pizzo di Casa (topped by a fire-watchtower) rises in front of you.

Just past the brow, leave the gravel road and go through the OPENING in the FENCE to the right. Following the sign 'SENTIERO PIANO TRAMONTANA', take the path up the slope. Coming level with a holm oak *(Quercus ilex)* with five trunks (1080m/3543ft; **55min**), turn right. This path rapidly zigzags up the steep slope, crosses an area with reddish limestone and reaches a small SADDLE. You go through a GATE and reach the higher alpine pastures. The buildings of the Rifugio Alpe Cucco lie below, in the valley on the right.

On no clear path, head west along the RIDGE, keeping to the left of the CREST. While the slopes descending gently to the south are used as pastures, the northern escarpment of Rocca Busambra drops vertically. From a distinctive RISE on the crest (1400m/4593ft; **1h45min**) you already have an excellent view. *Less experienced walkers should turn back at this point.* Experienced mountaineers should continue along the crest in the same direction, crossing rocky terrain. Some easy clambering over rocks is necessary. After crossing a SADDLE you reach the peak of **Rocca Busambra**

(1613m/5291ft; **2h45min**), marked by a trig point. The prominent position of Rocca Busambra offers views over wide parts of Sicily on a clear day. In the north, the Bosco della Ficuzza with the hunting castle lies at your feet; in the west you can see your route continuing along the ridge towards Rocca Ramusa. *Only those with time to spare and an adventurous spirit should continue!*

From the next SADDLE — where you can look north down to the Colonia Montana F.S. (holiday retreat of the State Railroad) — cross the slope to the left of the crest, without losing height. The route leads over big slabs of rock and negotiates a number of grazing fences with no stiles or gates. A deeply-cut valley separates Rocca Busambra from Rocca Ramusa (with a cross at the top). The path curves to the right (1150m/3773ft; **4h30min**) and descends across a meadow in the bottom of the valley, where rock walls rise steeply on both sides. Then bushes start to hem you in. On the way down, keep left and follow a cattle-path into the woods. The path swings north and runs alternately through woods and past fields. Above the **Fonte Ramusa** you meet a gravel road (828m/2716ft; **5h**).

Ficuzza is left. Turn right towards the Rifugio Alpe Cucco, through the dense oak wood at the foot of Rocca Busambra. When you reach a JUNCTION above the Colonia Montana F.S., turn right. With a clear view to Rocca Busambra and the Bosco della Ficuzza, the gravel road brings you back to the **Rifugio Alpe Cucco** (**6h10min**).

View from the Rifugio Alpe Cucco to Rocca Busambra, with yellow-flowering giant fennel (Ferula communis) in the foreground

Walk 32: MONTI DI PALAZZO ADRIANO

Distance: 11.5km/7.1mi; 3h45min

Grade: moderate walk on signed nature trails and gravel tracks. Ascent and corresponding descent of 440m/1444ft

Equipment: hiking boots, food and water bottle (you will find water en route)

How to get there and return: Head south from Palazzo Adriano (Car tour 6), passing the Pietra Salamone. Follow the signs 'Riserva Naturale Orientata Monti di Palazzo Adriano e Valle del Fiume Sosio' and park in front of the Visitors' Centre

at the Portella di Gebbia. Palazzo Adriano can also be reached by AST 🚌 from Palermo (www. astsicilia.it).

Note: The friendly owners of the *agriturismo* Casale di Borgia (Contrada Favara di Borgia, tel.: 0918348774, mobile: 3389274201, www.casaledi borgia.it) organise accommodation and nature excursions in this area. Palazzo Adriano is the seat of the Parco dei Monti Sicani Nature Reserve, created in 2012.

View towards Prizzi from Cozzo di Pietra Fucile

Palazzo Adriano lies on the northern slopes of Monti Sicani, deep in the Sosio Valley. The small town and surrounding landscape are among the most beautiful in inland Sicily, and this walk will give you the bird's eye view. The main churches of two ethnic groups face each other in the Piazza Grande (Piazza Umberto I.). The Chiesa Maria SS. del Lume follows the Latin liturgy, while Greek Orthodox rites are celebrated in the Chiesa Maria SS. Assunta. The Sicilian film director Giuseppe Tornatore chose the village as the setting for his Oscar-winning *Cinema Paradiso*. Palazzo Adriano is as inviting in reality as it was in the film but, amazingly, it has not yet attracted a myriad of tourists. So you can enjoy this miraculous little place without the crowds. The village is, however, a Mecca for paleontologists. The Pietra dei Saracini, Pietra di Salamone and other limestone rocks in the surroundings contain a wealth of fossilised fauna from the early Permian period.

Start the walk at the back of the VISITORS' CENTER (995m/3264ft) at the **Portella di Gebbia**: go left on the trail signposted 'SENTIERO PIETRA FUCILE'. Above a small patch of woodland, the path quickly ascends over old grazing areas, with wide views to the north over the Pietra Salamone to Palazzo Adriano, the Sosio Valley and Prizzi. As the path crosses the plateau it bends left. The rock walls drop sheer on your right, so don't go too close to the edge! A group of boulders to your left forms the peak of **Cozzo di Pietra Fucile** (1151m/3776ft; **30min**). Follow the northern rim of the plateau, enjoying views all around. Then the path descends over slabs of rock to the left and meets a gravel track (1140m/3740ft; **45min**).

Continue uphill to the right, following the sign 'SENTIERO DELLE NIVIERE'. On the brow of the ridge (1180m/3871ft; **50min**) the 'SENTIERO DELLE CARBONAIE' branches off to the right — your way back later in the walk. For now keep straight on. At the next fork take the 'SENTIERO BEVAIO RAVANUSA' to the right, past the *pagghiaru* **Marcato Ravanusa**. Up until the 1950s shepherds used these anicent stone-built thatched shelters; nowadays the Forestry Commission maintains them.

At the next fork (1190m/3904ft; **1h**), a short detour leads down to the **Bevaio Ravanusa** (1160m/3806ft; **1h05min**), a trough with fresh drinking water. Retrace your steps and continue uphill, until you meet a crossing gravel track (1215m/3986ft; **1h20min**). Descend to the right, ignoring the track turning off to the left. Shortly afterwards you reach a junction on a SADDLE (1120m/3675ft; **1h35min**). A fire-watch tower stands on the ridge to the southwest.

Continue to the right, now on the northern slopes of **Pizzo Gallinaro**. While the gravel track gently descends in wide bends, take in views of Caltabelotta in the west, the Sosio Valley, Giuliana, Prizzi and Rocca Busambra to the north (Walk 31). Your immediate surroundings are brightened by wild rose bushes, hawthorns, rock roses and remnants of mixed oak forest. After a WOODEN BARRIER a broad gravel track crosses your route: the **Regia Trazzera** (885m/2904ft; **2h05min**),which connects Burgio with Palazzo Adriano. Go right and, after just a few hundred metres, turn right again, following the signposted 'SENTIERO DELLE CARBONAIE'.

After a few minutes you're in a clearing with a *pagghiaru* and a charcoal burning area, set up as exhibits. You will cross more clearings used for charcoal burning in this dense oak wood. In May peonies (*Paeonia mascula*) are in full bloom. The fast-ascending path leads partly over coarse gravel, and dry oak leaves may make the ground slippery too, so watch your footing.

Leaving the woods behind you reach the edge of a grassy plateau; the path runs southeast across it. Boulders in the shade of two wild pear trees make a nice resting place (1090m/3904ft; **2h55min**); the 50min-point of your outgoing walk is not far ahead. Back on the gravel track, turn left. Stay on this broad gravel track, circling anti-clockwise around **Cozzo di Pietra Fucile**. You pass another reconstructed *pagghiaru,* the **Marcato du Puzzu**, before regaining the VISITORS' CENTER at the **Portella di Gebbia** (**3h45min**).

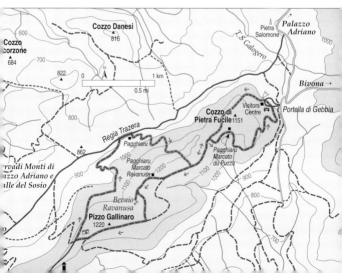

Walk 33: TORRE SALSA AND ERACLEA MINOA

Distance: The walk can be as long or as short as you like, there is no end to strolling along the beach. Allow at least 2h return.

Grade: easy walk in full sun; steps lead down to the beach. Perfect with kids! Ascent and corresponding descent of 160m/525ft

Equipment: light shoes, sun protection, binoculars, swimming things, food and water

How to get there and return: Exit the SS115 (Car tour 6) at km 159,700 and follow signs to the 'Riserva Naturale Torre Salsa'. After 2km turn off at the Visitors' Centre/Ingresso Omomorto on your right, and 🚗 park after another 400m at a junction with an information board/map for the nature reserve (www.wwftorresalsa.com). Treat yourself to a formidable meal and top-notch rooms at the Relais Briuccia (Via Trieste 1, mobile: 3397592176, www.relaisbriuccia.it) in nearby Monteallegro.

Note/Alternative walk: Don't miss the nearby Eraclea Minoa archaeological site (Car tour 6), with a small theatre, open from 09.00 until one hour before sunset. According to legend, the Cretan king Minos, in pursuit of Daedalus, set foot on Sicilian soil here and met his death. It is, however, true that Greeks from ancient Selinunte founded a town on the 'white cape' in the 6th century BC. The road continues down to the beach with the Sabbia d'Oro restaurant-bar, open all year. Heading west along the shore, you reach Capo Bianco without any difficulty. To round the cape to reach the estuary of the Fiume Platani, you must take off your shoes and wade across. The forestry commission has set up some reed huts on the opposite shore of the river, for water fowl observation. The estuary and the dunes are protected as a nature reserve. Return to the Bar Sabbia d'Oro the same way (1h30min). Another worthwhile excursion leads to the so-called Cala dei Turchi ('Turks' Staircase'), a blazing white marl cliff in the shape of a staircase south of Realmonte and west of Porto Empedocle.

T he Torre Salsa Nature Reserve and the adjacent beach of Eraclea Minoa with the striking Capo Bianco further to the west are among the last pristine stretches of coast in the province of Agrigento. Dazzling white cliffs of gypsum, marl and soft limestone jutt out into the sea, cupping large bays with golden beaches. Sometimes, in June and July, loggerhead turtles (*Caretta caretta*) deposit their eggs in the sand. The estuaries of the Torrente Salso and the Fiume Platani are a haven for water fowl and migrating birds.

Start the walk at the INFORMATION BOARD (140m/459ft) 400m west of the Omomorto Visitors' Centre. Follow the gently ascending gravel road to the south, indicated by the sign 'SENTIERO F. GALIA'. A steppe of grass tufts, low rosemary shrubs, wild thyme and dwarf fan palms cover the vast plateau. Wherever rock surfaces, gypsum crystals glitter in the sun. The view stretches as far as the white cliffs of Capo Bianco near Eraclea Minoa to the west.

At the next JUNCTION (160m/525ft;

118

10min), turn right. No settlements or buildings are in sight anywhere, only the odd vineyard or olive grove. The gently descending track leads across an unpaved parking area (70m/230ft; **25min**). Approaching the cliff, the trail bends to the left. Following the edge you look down on deserted beaches. The erosion results in bizarre shapes on the steep slopes. The 'SENTIERO NATURA' (60m/ft; **35min**) then descends a series of steps down to the beach (**45min**). Walk right along the coastline, at the foot of the cliffs. Flat, rocky promontories separate the individual bays. In shallow pools you can watch crabs and small fish trapped at low tide. Beyond the next cape (**1h**) the BEACH of **Torre Salsa** opens in a wide arc.

Return the same way to the junction/INFORMATION BOARD (**2h**).

Capo Bianco

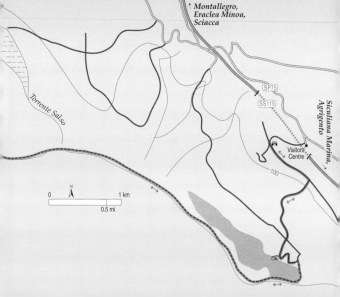

Walk 34: SANT'ANGELO MUXARO AND MONTE CASTELLO

Distance: 9km/5.6mi; 3h55min

Grade: moderate-strenuous walk along mule tracks and nature trails, with short sections on asphalted roads. Ascent and corresponding descent of 470m/1540ft

Equipment: hiking boots, sun protection, food and water

How get there and return: A 2km-long access road leads up from the SP19 (Car tour 6) to Sant'Angelo Muxaro. 🚗 park in the Piazza Umberto I in the village centre. Sant'Angelo Muxaro can be reached by public 🚌 from Agrigento/ Piazzale Rosselle (behind the post office; operator: LATTUCA, tel.: 092236125, www.autolineelattuca.it) and from Palermo/Via Balsamo (near the railway station; operator CUFARO, tel.: 0922916349, www.cuffaro.info). Private accommodation and guided tours can be arranged in Sant'Angelo through Pierfilippo Spoto and Val di Kam (Piazzo Umberto I 31, tel.: 0922919670, mobile: 3395305989, www.valdikam.it).

Shorter walk: Follow the main walk, but omit the ascent to Monte Castello (3km/2mi; 1h15min).

Note: By appointment (book at least a day ahead) the Ufficio della Riserva (Via Messina 2, tel.: 0922919749, www.legambienteriserve.it) arranges free speleo- logical tours in the Grotta Ciavuli, a gypsum cave. The tour is run by experienced guides, and you would be given the proper equipment.

Lying at the top of a plateau, Sant'Angelo Muxaro dominates the middle reaches of the Platani Valley. It is thought that nearby Monte Castello may have been the site of legendary Kamikos, capi- tal of the Sicanians in ancient times. Findings in the Bronze Age graves document close connections with Mycenae.

Start the walk at the **Piazza Umberto I**, in the heart of Sant' Angelo Muxaro (335m/1099ft). Walk north downhill on Via Libertà, and turn left at the BAR EDEN. Follow Via E. Fermi, then Via Matarella out of town. At a junction (315m/1033ft; **10min**), turn right on a mule track. Across the Platani Valley you can see S. Biagio Platani, and Monte Castello rises in front of you. Steps hewn in the glittering gypsum rock lead you down the slope, to a cross-track (200m/656ft; **30min**). This sweeps left towards the Bronze Age graves and will be your ongoing route on the return from Monte Castello.

For the moment follow the concreted track, descending to the right, until you meet a crossing asphalted road down in the **Vallone Ponte** (180m/591ft; **35min**). Follow it uphill to the left and, at the next junction, continue straight ahead. The road leads across a bridge. After the steep ascent, turn right on a gravelled forestry track (305m/1001ft; **1h05min**). Some Bronze Age burial niches are hewn in the rock wall to your left.

The forestry track leads through a eucalyptus grove and onto the SADDLE (345m/1132ft; **1h10min**) between Pizzo dell'Aquila and Monte Castello. Follow the main track straight ahead and turn right at the next fork. Leave the track before it descends any further, and turn right again on a track that is wide at the outset (305m/1001ft; **1h20min**). You cross a FIREBREAK, pass a plantation of cypresses and reach a small SADDLE, from where you see S. Biagio Platani to the north. Take a few steps to the right, until you can also see Sant' Angelo Muxaro to the east (330m/1083ft; **1h30min**). From this

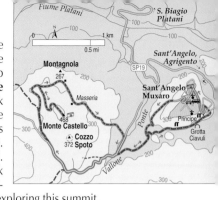

small PLATEAU follow the narrow path above the cypresses. It takes you up the western flank of **Monte Castello**, to the peak (468m/1535ft; **2h**). The ruins of an old fortress stand on the summit ridge. The panorama is beautiful. The brittle gypsum rock walls drop almost vertically, so take care when exploring this summit.

Return the same way to the PLATEAU at the 1h30min-point (**2h25min**) and descend the valley hollow to your right. Level with the first RUIN (260m/853ft; **3h35min**), the path heads right. The path passes below an abandoned *masseria*. At the fork take the broader track to the left, down to an asphalt road (165m/541ft; **3h**). Ascend to the right and return to the junction at the bottom of the western slope of Sant'Angelo (the 30min-point in your outward route; **3h10min**). Now follow the track leading straight ahead, gently uphill. Some of the Bronze Age graves you pass on your way consist of just a single room hewn in the living rock; their shape brings Mycenaean graves to mind. A stone bed was the last resting place of the dead. Some graves have an ante-room, the largest with a diameter of almost 9m/30ft (Tomba del Principe). Excavations brought a number of valuable burial gifts to light, which confirmed strong links with the Mycenaean world. There is a golden bowl from Sant'Angelo in the British Museum, richly decorated with bulls.

On the way a path branches off to right to the **Grotta Ciavuli**. A few paces further on, the track crosses the access road up to Sant'Angelo (235m/771ft; **3h25min**). Use the cobbled *mulattiera* as a short-cut. When you meet the road for the second time, follow it a short way to the left, to see the most spectacular of the tombs: a short detour leads to the **Tomba del Principe** (275m/902ft; **3h40min**). Back on the road, follow it uphill and, at the entrance to the village, turn left on Via Marconi. You pass the Chiesa dell'Itria before coming back to the **Piazza Umberto I. (3h55min)**.

Sant'Angelo Muxaro and Monte Castello

Walk 35: CACCAMO AND MONTE S. CALOGERO

Distance: 8km/5mi; 4h

Grade: strenuous walk, which requires some sense of orientation. Tracks, nature trails and rocky paths underfoot. Ascent and corresponding descent of 490m/1610ft

Equipment: hiking boots, sun protection, windproofs, food and water

How to get there and return: From the crossroads at the southeastern entrance to Caccamo (Car tour 6), level with the Bar del Carmine, turn left on Via S. Vito. The road leads steeply uphill past a modern block of flats. The road then narrows and (only partly asphalted from now on) heads towards Monte S. Calogero. After passing under the power line, turn the car round and 🚗 park on a rounded hilltop, 4km/2.5mi beyond Caccamo. Accommodation in the historical centre of Caccamo and surroundings c/o Vacanze Caccamo, Corso Umberto I. 10, tel.: 0918121314, mobile: 3803484661, www.vacanzecaccamo.it. Caccamo can also be reached by public 🚌 from Palermo/Via Balsamo (near the railway station; operator RANDAZZO, tel.: 0918148235, http://autobusrandazzo. altervista.org).

Monte S. Calogero, rising almost vertically more than 1300m/4265ft from the coastal plain, is the unchallenged kingdom of birds of prey or the adventurous hikers who climb to the summit. Coming from inland, the ascent is a bit easier, but for all that, the mountain doesn't lose its majesty. Caccamo is a small town well worth visiting. The 14th-century castle of the Chiaramonte (open daily from 09.30-12.00 and 13.30-18.30) is among the largest, best preserved and most beautiful in Sicily.

Start the walk from the ROUNDED HILLTOP (835m/2740ft) where you parked the car: follow the gravel track heading northeast. It runs between barbed-wire fences and past fields and pastures. To your right is the rocky ridge which culminates in the peak of Monte S. Calogero in front of you. After a few minutes views open up left towards the sea, Capo Zafferano and Monte Pellegrino (Walk 24). Along the way you pass through a number of GATES. Turn right at a FORK (830m/2723ft; **20min**), following a sign, 'M. S. CALOGERO'. The (initially) gently-rising track crosses a pasture and passes through more GATES. It then becomes a rather stony cattle trail, leading

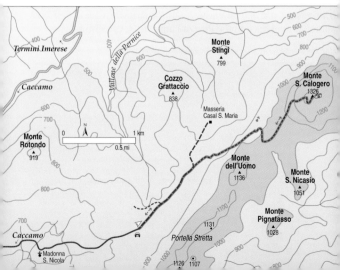

Monte S. Calogero from the west

picturesquely between boulders, tree spurge and holm oaks. Across the roofs of the Masseria Casal S. Maria, you look down on Termini Imerese. At a FAINT JUNCTION (960m/3150ft; **40min**), take the path to the right, zigzagging uphill. Crossing the notch below **Monte dell'Uomo**, the faint path takes you through trees and boulders, then swings back northeast, onto a STONY PLATEAU (1020m/3346ft; **50min**). *Remember this spot for the way back!*

With the peak of Monte S. Calogero ahead, look out for boulders with RED PAINT WAYMARKS. Keeping in the same direction, with a tree-covered hill to your right and a rock face to your left, step over a barbed wire fence and follow the valley uphill. Wild pear trees (*Pyrus piraster*), blooming exuberantly in spring, dot the pastures. Once you reached a SECOND, HIGHER PLATEAU (1090m/3346ft; **1h**), you can make out the further route to the peak on the western flank of the mountain. From a notch with a copse of holm oaks (*Quercus ilex*) the path swings east (FADED RED MARKINGS indicate the route as it ascends over rock rubble) and then bends to the north. The views stretch far to the west, with Rocca Busambra (Walk 31) as a distinctive landmark. You reach a small TERRACE (1205m/3953ft; **1h30min**) from where you can look down on the harbour of Termini Imerese.

The final part of the ascent begins here. Climb the old pilgrims' trail, partly secured by retaining walls, which leads up to the ruined chapel of S. Calogero. As the trail rises, you look down on Cerda (a place where you can eat excellent artichokes in spring), while the massif of the Madonie Mountains unfolds to the east. Cefalù stands out because of its prominent castle rock (Walk 19). On the SUMMIT of **Monte S. Calogero** (1326m/4350ft; **2h**), the foundation walls of the little chapel stand beside a modern antenna. On a clear day you are rewarded with one of the most beautiful panoramas in all of Sicily.

Descend the same way and return to your starting point at the HILLTOP (**4h**).

Walk 36: PAPYRUS ALONG THE CIANE

See photograph pages 12-13 **Distance:** 5.5km/3.4mi; 2h

Grade: easy, almost level walk, on partly overgrown and sometimes muddy nature trails. *Reaching the source of the Ciane depends on trail maintenance!*

Equipment: light hiking boots, food and water (good picnic spots; Picnic 23)

How to get there and return: From Syracuse (Car tour 8) take the SS115 towards Cassibile. Once you've crossed the bridges over the Ciane River and the Mammaiabica Canal, turn right on the small road running parallel with the canal. Cross the railway line and 🚗 park at the bridge over the canal where the road is closed to traffic. *Or,* to reach the source of the Ciane, take the SP14 towards Canicattini and turn off left on the SR3, following the brown signs 'Fonte Ciane'. 🚗 park after 3km at a wooden kiosk, where the entrance drive to the *agriturismo* Villa dei Papiri (tel.: 0931721321, www.villadeipapiri.it) is ahead. There is plenty of accommodation in Syracuse. I particularly recommend the Hotel Gutkowski, Lungomare Vittorini 26, tel.: 0931465861, www.guthotel.it.

Starting out as a limestone spring, the Ciane's short meanders empty into the Porto Grande at Syracuse. The exotic vegetation along its banks makes this little river, shown on pages 12-13, very interesting. Nowhere else in Sicily or the Mediterranean will you see so much papyrus growing naturally. The plant was introduced on Sicily in ancient times by the Ptolemies, who made a gift of it to the Siracusan tyrant Hieron II. Try to visit the Ciane in early morning or late afternoon, as there is more birdlife.

Start the walk by crossing the BRIDGE (5m/16ft) over the **Mammaiabica Canal** and heading north for 160m/yds to another BRIDGE, this one over the **Ciane River** (5m/16ft; **5min**; sign: 'Riserva naturale Fiume Ciane e Saline di Siracusa'). Don't cross the bridge; take the path heading left beside the river. Papyrus grows in thick clumps on the banks. After a pleasant stroll you come to an old MOORING (6m/20ft; **15min**; Picnic 23), a pleasant spot for a picnic in the half-shade of tall ash trees — the loveliest spot on the walk!

A few steps further upstream you encounter the first of FOUR ARCHED BRIDGES. Keep to the southern side of the river; if the path has been cleared, you should be able to reach the FOURTH BRIDGE (8m/26ft; **50min**). Cross it and follow the trail marked with wooden poles, to a circular pool, the SOURCE OF THE **Ciane** (8m/26ft; **1h**).

Then retrace your steps to your car (**2h**).

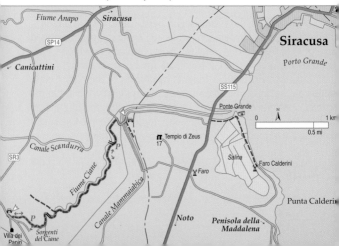

Walk 37: NOTO ANTICA AND THE CAVA DEL CAROSELLO

Distance: 5km/3mi; 1h40min
Grade: moderate walk on gravel roads and partly overgrown nature trails
Equipment: hiking boots, swimwear, food, water

How to get there and return: Drive via S. Corrado di Fuori and S. Maria delle Scala. 🚗 park at the Porta della Montagna (Car tour 8). Several places in Noto let rooms, for instance Al Canisello, a villa in the west of the old town, Via Pavese 1, tel.: 0931835793, mobile: 3203731 932, www.villacanisello.it.

Shorter walk: From the Porta della Montagna walk back along the asphalt road a short way. Before the bridge crosses the Salitello, turn left on a path. This leads to the Grotta del Carciofo, a Jewish cave-tomb from imperial Roman times; the seven-armed candelabrum carved into the rock reminded later visitors of an artichoke (*carciofo*). The Grotta delle Cento Bocche, an early Christian necropolis, is also interesting (500m/ yds; 15min).

Noto Antica is situated on the heart-shaped plateau of Monte Alveria. The advantages of this natural fortress were discovered in ancient times. Siculic, Greek and Roman necropoli testify to continuous settlement here since the 9th century BC. During the Spanish period, Noto was regarded as an impregnable fortress. In 1500 King Ferdinand the Catholic had the following inscription placed on the Porta della Montagna: 'NETUM INGENOSA. URBS NUN-QUAM VI CAPTA'. In the end Noto was not taken by enemy armies, but by a terrible earthquake: on January 10th, 1693, it crushed the town to the ground overnight. A new Noto was built further to the south on the slopes of the Meti, a model of a rationally-planned baroque town. Today a quiet peace lies over the deserted ruins.

The walk begins at the **Porta della Montagna** (428m/1404ft), where a panel with an overview map shows a plan of Noto Antica. A gravel road leads through the impressive town gate into the area of the ruined city. Only the bastions and the Torre Reale were able to withstand the tremendous force of the earthquake. Follow the level gravel road past the Torre Reale, a round tower from the Angevin era. You pass the overgrown ruins of houses, palaces and churches, and come to a JUNCTION (415m/1362ft; **15min**), where a SHRINE TO SAINT MARY commemorates the devastating earthquake. (Descending to the right here, you could short-cut to the 30min-point in the walk.) Continue straight ahead for another 500m/yds on the narrowing gravel road, then turn right and follow the cart track through the gap in the wall (415m/1362ft; **20min**). (The road continues ahead for another 300m/yds to the Eremo di S. Maria della Providenza, not visible from here.)

In less than 200m/yds you reach an open field (though you may not see it if the vegetation is high). Follow the cart ruts north across the pasture, passing through another gap in a drystone wall. After the SECOND GAP (405m/1329ft; **30min**) a track, coming down from the junction at the 15 min-point, joins from the right. Turn left at this point and climb over the STILE. You're outside the old city walls

now. Oleander, poplars and fig-trees line the stream, and you enjoy a bird's-eye view over the gorge from the ledge. Follow the path to the right, down into the canyon, the **Cava del Carosello**. Broad steps hewn in the limestone lead past an ANCIENT GUARD HOUSE dug into the rock. At the BOTTOM OF THE VALLEY (325m/1066ft; **40min**) the crystal clear stream forms little pools, some big enough for a dip — heaven on a hot day!

Explore the valley floor at your leisure. The Syracuse Forestry Commission 'rediscovered' this long-forgotten corner of the Iblei Mountains in 2008, and since then has been working to rebuild the old muletrack network for hikers. Most striking are the TANNERIES dug into the rock face, dating back at least to the Renaissance. They are very like the Morroccan tanneries in the city of Fes.

You *could* retrace your steps from here to the Porta della Montagna, but it is more interesting to continue

Tanneries in the Cava del Carosello

upriver, past many more tanneries. Up until the end of the 17th century, the Cava del Carosello must have been the site of a thriving leather industry. Cross the river to the left and continue upstream. After a copse of eucalyptus, ascend the trail to the left, now passing a series of FLOUR MILLS. One of the mills lies in a man-made cave to the left (345m/1132ft; **1h**). The trail broadens out now.

Don't miss the turn off to the right after a couple of hundred metres! After crossing the dry valley floor, the path ascends in the shadow of Mediterranean maquis and goes through a GAP in a wall (395m/1296ft; **1h15min**). Beyond the gap you meet a crossing *mulattiera*, which you follow downhill to the right. You cross another dry valley floor (with an ANIMAL FEEDING PLACE cut into the rock) and rise again. Climb over a STILE (415m/1362ft; **1h30min**), turn sharp left beyond the remains of a wall, and re-enter Noto Antica. The gravel path leads back to the **Porta della Montagna** (**1h40min**).

Walk 38: THE VENDICARI NATURE RESERVE

See photograph page 41

Distance: 15km/9.3mi; 4h 15min

Grade: easy, almost level walk on nature trails

Equipment: trekking sandals (ideal for crossing wet areas), sun protection, bathing things, binoculars, food and water

How to get there and return: 9km south of Noto a cul-de-sac road turns off the SP19 between Noto and Pachino to the 'Riserva Naturale Orientata di Vendicari' (Car tour 8). The road ends after 1.3km in front of a barrier at the main entrance to the reserve. 🚗 park here. The AST public 🚌 line (www.aziendasilianatrasporti.it) runs on the SP19 between Noto and Pachino and stops on request at the turn-off to Vendicari. In the immediate proximity of the reserve is the *agriturismo* Il Roveto, an 18th-century baroque manor house, mobile: 3387426343, www.roveto.it. There is also accommodation in Noto (see Walk 37) and Noto Marina.

Longer walk: From Calamosche you can walk on to the estuary of the Tellaro. If the water is not too high, you can wade across the river. The ruins of ancient Eloro lie on the opposite shore. Return to Calamosche the same way (adds 4km/2.5mi; 1h30min).

Notes: On request, you can be accompanied by park rangers, who will point out the different bird species. It is forbidden to leave the official trail, and swimming at the large sandy beach might be restricted in particular seasons (when the birds are breeding in the dunes or on the sand, or when loggerhead turtles are depositing their eggs). Don't miss the Roman Villa del Tellaro a short detour off the SP19!

More than eight kilometres of untouched sand and rock coast stretch out before you on this walk. Vendicari is one of the most important migration bases in the Mediterranean. Its *pantani*, the lagoons, dry out in the summer and fill again with rainwater in winter. Vendicari is not only a paradise for birds, but also for birdwatchers. More than 230 species have been identified here to date. With a little bit of luck you can see flamingos in all seasons.

The walk begins at the MAIN ENTRANCE TO THE RESERVE, where a short walkway takes you past the Pantano Grande (big lagoon) and abandoned salt-pans. On reaching the shore (**7min**), you meet the main trail. This runs the whole length of the reserve, parallel with the coast. For conservation reasons, it is forbidden to walk across the fragile dune habitat, so this is the only place to cross the dune belt and reach the long sandy beach which is punctuated by the Torre di Vendicari to the north. The Isola Vendicari lies off the Punta d'Isola. There are strong currents in the bay so, even if it looks tempting, you would be wise *not* to try swimming out to the island.

The **Torre di Vendicari** (**15min**) was built in the 15th century to defend the port against corsair attacks. Noto shipped large quantities of grain, carob and almonds out of the port of Vendicari. The chimney of the *tonnara* rises on the coast, next to the tower (see photograph on page 41). Until the 1940s, tuna was caught and tinned here. Fish-processing has been going on in Vendicari for thousands of years. Below the old workers' accommodation, you can still recognise basins hewn out of the rock: in antiquity fish was salted in these basins and the fish remains processed to *garum,* a strongly-flavoured seasoning paste much relished as a component of almost every Roman dish.

The way continues above the rugged, rocky shore, edged at the left by one of the typical drystone walls. A loose garrigue of pleasantly-scented broom *(Calicotome spinosa),* mastic trees *(Pistacia lentiscus)* and dwarf fan palms *(Chamaerops humilis)* surrounds you. You pass the ruins of the GUARDIA DI FINANZA (barracks) and shortly afterwards a small BIRD-WATCHING HUT (**35min**). Beyond the Pantano Piccolo, you can see the city of Noto on the hills. By now the trail is following the course of the ancient Via Elorina, which connected Syracuse with Eloro and went on to Camarina. Old cart ruts are still recognisable in the rock. The trail leads across a little hill, the **Cozzo Balsamo**. Thyme bushes cover the stony soil, their perfume filling the air. At the point where a wide track leads away from the coast, follow the narrow path straight ahead (**55min**). After another hillock, the path descends to **Calamosche** (**1h10min**), a hidden bay with a lovely sandy beach.

Passing the *tonnara* again, return to the **Pantano Grande** (**2h10min**). To explore the southern part of the reserve, follow the trail along the shore of the **Pantano Roveto**. The dune belt to your left is covered by juniper bushes. Depending on the water-level, you may have to wade through the outflow of the Pantano Roveto. Then an unmarked path off right leads you up a little hill to the **Citadella dei Maccari** (18m/59ft; **3h10min**). Some necropoli and a little church, with its dome still intact, are the only survivors of the Byzantine settlement that stood here in the 6-7th centuries.

Return the same way to the ENTRANCE TO THE RESERVE (**4h15min**).

Walk 39: SCICLI AND THE COLLE DI SAN MATTEO

Distance: 2.5km/1.6mi; 50min

Grade: easy walk on cobbled lanes and gravel roads. Ascent and descent of 100m/330ft

Equipment: stout shoes, food and water

How to get there and return: 🚗 park in Scicli, in the Piazza Italia (Car Tour 8). Compagnia del Mediterraneo

can help with accommodation in and around Scicli (Via Dei Lillà 56, mobile: 3920590023, www.compagniadelmediterraneo.it).

Scicli is a little-known baroque jewel. You can combine a visit to this small town with a short walk up Colle di San Matteo. The views are lovely, and the place is perfect for a picnic.

The walk begins at the **Piazza Italia** (115m/377ft). With your back to the Chiesa S. Ignazio, turn into Via S. Bartolomeo, with the richly-decorated balconies of the Palazzo Fava on your right. You pass the church of S. Bartolomeo (with an interesting nativity crib) on your left. The cobbled Via Guadagna then starts to lead you up the **Cava S. Bartolomeo**. At the point where this stream bed becomes visible, turn left on the narrow Via Ripida (**10min**).

Steps take you quickly up between the houses, then the alley (now called Via Timpanello) continues above the rooftops. Paths branch off right and left to cave dwellings, which were lived in up until the 1950s; in some places you can still see limestone rocks black from soot. The main trail ascends between drystone walls where capers (*Caparis spinosa*) grow out of the crevices. Below the castle rock continue to the right. Soon you meet a concreted track (210m/689ft; **30min**), almost at the top of **Colle di San Matteo**. Descend to the left, passing the RUINS OF THE CASTLE on the crest of the ridge. The track leads behind the CHURCH OF **S. Matteo** onto a terrace (185m/607ft; **35min**). The panorama is marvellous, with Scicli spread at your feet.

From here cobbled Via Matteo takes you back into town. Cross the Piazza Dandolo and follow Via Matrice: this leads straight to the remarkably eccentric baroque **Palazzo Beneventano** (**45min**). Turn left in front of the Palazzo; it's just a few steps back to the **Piazza Italia** (**50min**).

The town of Scicli spreads out below the Colle di San Matteo.

Walk 40: RAGUSA IBLA AND THE CAVA DELLA MISERICORDIA

Distance: 10km/6.2mi; 4h30min

Grade: moderate walk on old mule trails and forestry tracks. Ascent and corresponding descent of 200m/650ft. **NB:** After heavy rain it may not be possible to cross the Cava San Leonardo or Cava della Misericordia, as there are only stepping stones.

Equipment: stout shoes, food and water bottle (there is a a spring en route)

How to get there and return: 🚗 park in Ragusa (Car tour 8), off Corso Italia in the Piazza Mateotti — or park in the Piazza della Repubblica and start the walk at the 20min-point. There are good hotels of various categories in Ragusa, including Le Stanze del Sole (Via Armando Diaz 15, tel.: 0932686282, mobile: 3683179601, www.lestanzedelsole.it). The friendly owners organise gided trekking tours in the vicinity. To indulge in the life of rural nobility, stay at the five-star Eremo della Giubiliana off the road to Marina di Ragusa (tel.: 0932669119, www.eremodellagiubiliana.it). Public 🚌 between Ragusa Ibla and Ragusa, operator AST (www.astsicilia.it).

A visit to Ragusa Ibla, one of the most beautiful baroque towns in southeastern Sicily, is a must. On this short walk you will see for yourself how wonderfully the old Ibla fits into the landscape. The new Ragusa, on the plateau, was completely rebuilt after the devastating earthquake in 1693.

The walk begins at the **Piazza Mateotti** (490m/1608ft) in Ragusa. Follow Corso Italia, then Via XXIV. Maggio downhill. From the BELVEDERE above the Chiesa S. Maria delle Scale, descend the many steps until you reach the **Piazza della Repubblica** (395m/ 1296ft; **20min**) in Ragusa Ibla. After taking a good look at the Chiesa del Purgatorio and the Palazzo Cosentini with its grotesque balconies, descend the narrow stepped Discesa San Leonardo, past the public toilets. Leave the town through an ARCHWAY, with the Cava San Leonardo in front of you. A path leads down into the valley and you cross the **San Leonardo** on STEPPING STONES (335m/ 1099ft; **25min**).

On the opposite side of the river, follow the gravel track to the left for a few metres/yards, then turn right on an old mule track (initially cobbled). Climbing between walls and past carob and olive groves, you quickly gain height on the north side of the valley. The ascent then continues more gently; a small tributary of the San Leonardo lies to your right. After passing an isolated house, you reach a small asphalted square, where a road ends and cars can turn round (**45min**). If you want to shorten the walk, you can turn right here and find a pleasant picnic spot with views to Ragusa Ibla.

To continue the walk, follow the asphalt road just a short way uphill. Before the roads bends

View from Ragusa to Ragusa Ibla, with the Cava S. Leonardo to the left

to the right and rises further, turn left on a concreted track (440m/1444ft; **50min**), down into the canyon, called **Cava Mulini** in this section. After a steep descent, the now-gravelled forestry road gently rises again. Abandoned orchards and the many RUINED MILLS in the valley tell of intense use in the past.

Beyond a SPRING (415m/1362ft; **1h10min**), you pass through a GREEN IRON GATE of the Forestry Commission. Ignore minor tracks branching off right, down to the stream, but turn right on the trail signed 'N° 721 — SENTIERO DEGLI EREMITI' (515m/1690ft; **1h50min**). This takes you down to the stream bed (now called Cava de la Misericordia; 505m/1657ft; **2h**). A giant laurel (*Laurus nobilis*) casts its shadow over a pool. Walk 10m/yds upstream, to where you can cross on rock slabs (which can be very slippery!). On far side of the stream, steps take you up to a one-time HERMITAGE (520m/1706ft; **2h10min**), now a CAI refuge.

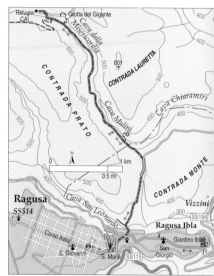

Explore the upper reaches of the **Cava della Misericordia** at leisure, then return the same way to the **Piazza della Re-pubblica** in **Ragusa Ibla** (**4h**). While you're here, be sure to take the opportunity to visit the Duomo San Giorgio and the Giardino Ibleo (Picnic 26; photograph page 11). Then either catch a bus or retrace your steps to the **Piazza Mateotti** in **Ragusa** (**4h30min**).

Walk 41: PANTALICA

Distance: 13km/8mi; 3h45min

Grade: moderate walk along nature trails, gravel roads and a short stretch on an asphalted road. Ascent and corresponding descent of 500m/1640ft

Equipment: hiking boots, sun protection, swimming things, food and water

How to get there and return: From Ferla, follow the signs for 'Pantalica' and after 11km 🚗 park below the Anaktoron (Car tour 8). (On the way, look out for signs 'Agriturismo Porta Pantalica' (mobile: 3313864354, www.portapantalica.it), a good place to sleep and eat.) Coming from Sortino, follow the signs 'Pantalica' and after 8km 🚗 park at the end of the asphalt road.

Shorter walks: The suggested walk can be split up into several shorter walks. For instance, you could walk from the Anaktoron as described below to the necropolis of Filiporto and then return the same way (4km/2.5mi; 1h). The Calcinara Valley is very beautiful. When coming from Ferla, drive up to the end of the asphalt road and walk down left to the valley. Coming from Sortino, drive to the end of the asphalt road and follow the route described below down to the Calcinara. *Note: some of the signposts mentioned in the text may be missing.*

The tree spurge (Euphorbia dendroides) *in the Anapo Valley shines bright red in summer.*

For 500 years Pantalica was the centre and capital of the most important Bronze Age civilisation in Sicily. Unfortunately, apart from the Anaktoron and the necropoli, no ancient building has survived. The more than 5000 cave-tombs, which perforate the bright limestone rock like honeycombs, date principally from the 13th to the 8th century BC. Some of the more important excavation finds are displayed in the archaeological museum at Syracuse. Dramatic canyons, luxuriant vegetation, and clear rivers make this walk a great experience of nature, as well as history.

The walk begins at the CAR PARK below the **Anaktoron**. A few steps take you up to the little RISE (415m/1362ft). A wooden fence protects the foundation walls of the Anaktoron, a palace dating from the Bronze Age. Follow the signposted trail to the east, towards 'NECROPOLI DI FILIPORTO' and 'S. MICIDARIO'. The path descends in a curve to the right and heads back west. When you come to some large CHAMBER TOMBS (9-8th century BC), another path joins from below (**5min**); this will be your return route later in the walk. Continue straight ahead, with the canyon of the Anapo to your left. Along the way you pass steps descending to the 'BELVEDERE NECROPOLI SUD' (**20min**). Before you walk down these steps, keep ahead to see the Byzantine rock church of S. Micidario and the necropolis of Filiporto. **S. Micidario** is surrounded by a small village of cave-dwellings. A few minutes later you reach the **Sella di Filiporto** (380m/1247ft; **30min**), where a defensive trench, which was originally hewn 7m/25ft deep in the rock, protected the ancient town from the west. The canyons of the Calcinara and Anapo offered natural protection from all other sides. You enjoy a magnificent view over the the **Necropoli di Filiporto** (9-8th century BC) to the Anapo Valley. After taking a break here, go back to the turn-off 'BELVEDERE NECROPOLI SUD' (**40min**). Rock steps take you steeply downhill to a FORK. Both branches go down to the bright gravel road, but the path to the left descends more gently. You reach the gravel road west of the former railway station (**1h**).

Turn left on the gravel road in the floor of the **Anapo Valley** and you come to the old PANTALICA RAILWAY STATION (229m/750ft; **1h05min**). Today the building is used as a natural history museum (adjacent toilets). A narrow-gauge railway which connected Syracuse with Vizzini ran along here until 1956. Immediately after the railway station take the gravel road to the right, crossing to the other side of the RIVER. Orchards cover the valley floor; huge ash trees, poplars, willows and planes grow along the water's edge. Shortly before the roads returns to the left bank, you pass a picnic area. Back on the old railway track, a path turns off to the left (SENTIERO N° 4) and climbs uphill towards the Anaktoron. Ignore it and continue along the gravel road, which leads through a short TUNNEL and across a BRIDGE. Before the next (long) tunnel, leave the gravel road and turn left on a path (200m/656ft; **1h30min**).

The path, initially accompanied by wooden railings, follows the

course of the Anapo. Past the CONFLUENCE of the Anapo and the Calcinara, you round the north side of the mountain. Shortly before the path meets the gravel road again, turn left (by a stand of aspens) and descend to the river. If the water level is not too high, you can cross the river here on STEPPING STONES, otherwise you must take off your shoes and wade through (195m/640ft; **1h55min**). From the opposite bank a path (soon widening to a track) ascends in hairpins and climbs past a deserted farmstead and through almond and carob groves. A LADDER STILE takes you over a fence and, on the far side, you meet the ASPHALT ROAD coming from Sortino (300m/984ft; **2h10min**).

Follow the road to the left; at first it is gravelled, then it narrows to a path and continues its descent between drystone walls. The canyon-like ravine of the Calcinara opens up in front of you. The cave-tombs of the Necropoli Nord-Ovest perforate the steep limestone rocks like honeycombs. You pass just beside some of these tombs. Looking closer, you can see that they were originally closed by stone slabs. Some of these richly-decorated limestone slabs are on show in the archaeological museum in Syracuse. Dozens of rock steps take you down to the floor of the **Calcinara** (235m/771ft; **2h40min**). From the end of May, the oleanders here will be in full bloom. The clear water of the river runs in small cascades over the rocks into little pools — one of which is just big enough for you to swim a few strokes.

Cross the STEPPING STONES to the far bank and climb the steps hewn in the rock. On the southern side of the valley, you can see the opening of the **Grotta dei Pipistrelli**, where hundreds of bats nest. From the VIEWPOINT above the 'NECROPOLI NORD-OVEST' the way leads round the spur, past another cave entrance (this one closed with a grid). You reach a little CAR PARK at the end of the asphalt road coming from Ferla (300m/984ft; **2h55min**). Follow this road for a while. Beyond the BRIDGE, a short cul-de-sac path leads left to the 'BELVEDERE DELLA CAVETTA'. After a couple of minutes, where the road bends sharp right (355m/1165ft; **3h05min**), leave it and walk straight ahead on a narrow path, descending in zigzags (partly over loose stones). You drop to a crossing path (285m/935ft; **3h15min**), which leads down to the old railway track in the Anapo Valley (SENTIERO N° 4). Continue climbing to the right, partly on rock steps. Rise to a crossing path and follow it left uphill. A few metres further on, at the next JUNCTION, go right (**3h30min**). (The path to the left leads to the Byzantine rock church S. Nicolicchio.

The main path takes you up to the T-junction below the large CHAMBER-TOMBS. Turn right here, back to the **Anaktoron** (**3h45min**).

Index